DIVORCELESS MARRIAGE

DIVORCELESS MARRIAGE

PUT IT
FIRST
— ♥ —
MAKE IT
LAST

Dr. Randy L. Bott

Millennial Press
Salt Lake City, Utah

Millennial Press, Inc.
11968 South Doves Landing Drive
Riverton, Utah 84065

Publisher's Cataloging-in-Publication Data
(Provided by Quality Books, Inc.)

Bott, Randy L., 1945—
    Divorceless marriage: put it first, make it last / by Randy L. Bott. — 1st ed.
    p. cm.
    Includes index.
    Preassigned LCCN: 97-74850
    ISBN 0-9660231-0-2

    1. Marriage. 2. Communication in the family. 3 Parenting.
I. Title.
HQ734.B68 1997   646.7'8
                                            QBI97-41296

This book is dedicated to my loving wife, Vickie, who has weathered the rough times, tolerated the growing seasons, and created the memories which make marriage enjoyable and doable. Much of what I have learned has been from our experiences in identifying problems and seeking for acceptable solutions. Since divorce has never been an option for either of us, we decided that living together in love and harmony was far more desirable than existing in a cold war atmosphere or in a living hell.

Thanks also to the countless couples who have provided insight into how these principles work in lives other than our own. The successes have verified the functionality of the principles. The struggles have motivated me to search deeper for elusive principles which work every time they are mutually applied.

Finally, thanks to you, the reader, who will discover for yourself that "living together in love" is not a myth nor a fantasy but can be a living reality. So my final dedication is to those couples who are dedicated to make divorceless marriage a way of life.

CONTENTS

— ♥ —

1

INTRODUCTION

—❤—

"The decree is final. Your divorce is complete. You are no longer 'husband and wife!'" A judge who doesn't even know either of you has just completed the shattering of your dreams. It didn't start with him and he didn't cause it, but by the authority vested in him by the State, he has just nullified your lifelong dream—to live happily ever after in a blissful marriage.

Can such a scene be avoided? If the answer is not an obvious "yes," there would be no need for this book. However, if you are expecting some "quick fix" or "cutesy solutions" to the challenging problems associated with "living happily ever after," perhaps this book is not what you are looking for. There are proven practices which, when consistently applied, greatly increase the likelihood that you will have a happy marriage. There are logical attitudes which tend towards harmony and stability when continually fostered. There are correct principles which eliminate from the marital pathway the stumbling blocks which seem so destructive to so many marriages. None of these things will work unless the two of you make them work. It will require that both partners be united in your quest to have a heavenly marriage. It will necessitate a tenacious attitude mutually shared to make your dreams come true. But when you decide to give it a try, you will be happily rewarded with a joyful marriage.

A few years ago I read an article by a rather prominent marriage therapist. In reciting her credentials for being classified as an expert on loving and marital relations, she said: "I have been married and divorced four times. I am currently divorced. I ought to qualify as an expert!" From my vantage point, she is the least qualified person to tell me and my wife how to "live happily ever after." By the age of 31, she had tried and failed four times and was not in a marriage relationship at the time.

Where do I get my credentials? My wife and I have been married twenty-seven years and have never had a fight! Don't misunderstand, we disagree all the time. She is a very strong-willed person and I have very definite ideas of my own. But we have learned how to disagree without fighting and arguing with each other. We are in the process of raising six children ranging in age from twenty-five years to twelve years. Three girls were born to our union and then three boys followed. Two of our oldest daughters are married and have moved away from home. The other four are present in the home to one degree or another. If you remember how much time you spent at home as a teenager, you will understand what I mean. We are not a perfect family but we have enjoyed relative peace and harmony through the years. The challenges associated with raising children (especially teenagers!) can put a lot of stress on a marriage. We have managed to keep the lines of communication open even during those stressful times without yelling and screaming at each other.

In order to satisfy the world's cry for credentials, I may mention that I have a doctor's degree in educational leadership which is a combination of educational administration and curriculum development. My undergraduate work was in psychology and I have been engaged in education and counseling for almost thirty years.

You will note from the onset that I do not quote extensively from the "experts." Although there are many volumes which have been written with excellent advice, just rehashing old ideas or readjusting thoughts within a chapter is not what I perceive we need. Therefore, I have tried to present fresh, new, workable ideas, some of which may be scorned and criticized by the experts. I am willing to stand the risk of being mocked by revealing to you the innermost secrets of our marriage. Let those who mock compare their marital happiness to ours and see if they can honestly say their ideas are superior. In saying this, I am not speaking disparagingly about the experts. I am saying that the best ideas have not been thought of, the best methods have not been devised, and the best results have not yet been achieved. If we set our sights too low in marriage and achieve our goal, will we in turn regret that we didn't shoot for something more lofty? I would much rather shoot for perfection and miss, falling a little bit short, than shoot for mediocrity and achieve it!

In the chapters of this book I intend to be as pragmatic as possible in sharing with you those things which have worked for us. I will also draw upon my nearly three decades as a professional educator for examples and lessons both experienced and observed. One cannot live long enough to make all the mistakes there are to make. It seems reasonable and profitable to learn from the mistakes of others and avoid learning everything in the school of hard knocks. Even when mistakes are made, they don't need to be lethal to your marriage if you are willing to learn from them. Continually making the same mistake without correcting the cause seems counterproductive at best and reflective of poor judgment and diminished understanding at worst.

Although the thoughts expressed in these chapters have been successful for us and many others, they may require modification to fit your individual personalities and circumstances. In other words, one solution may not fit all problems. Be creative. Try the principles presented in the chapters. Talk about them between the two of you. Adopt before you adapt. Give a diligent try and see if the principle works for you before you revise, modify, or discard it.

The story is told of a very successful trapper who decided to retire and sell his business to a young apprentice who had worked with him for several years. The old man carefully instructed the young trapper on where to set the traps and how to arrange the bait to insure the greatest success. After months of not hearing from the young man, the old trapper returned in the spring to assess the progress. To his surprise the cabin was vacant and the young man had gone. Assuming the old man would come by to check on him, the young trapper had left a note of explanation. He lamented how the beaver had mysteriously disappeared at the same time the old man left. He explained that he had evaluated the methods the old trapper had taught him and discovered many flaws in his trapping plan which he had immediately corrected. After several months of little or no success he had concluded that the beaver population had been depleted and had struck out in search of a more lucrative profession.

It doesn't take long for one to see the moral of the story. He had taken a thriving, successful business and by changing just a few things had successfully destroyed the business. To his dying day the young trapper will probably blame the failure of the business on the retired trapper's old-fashioned methods or to the demise of the beaver population. So it is with so many marriages. Marriages do not fail because the institution is bad or because "nobody lives happily ever after any more." Marriages fail because proven, time-honored principles are altered or replaced with the latest popular craze or most recently accepted sociological theory.

If we want to increase the chances of marital success, perhaps we should look to the older couples who have lived together for many years and see what they do and how they do it. New isn't always better. Activity is often mistaken for progress. A change is not always an improvement. Especially in marriage, this time-worn adage is applicable: "If it ain't broke, don't fix it. If it is broke, don't leave until it's fixed!"

As we turn our attention to the principles necessary in building a divorce-less marriage, it is advisable to consider the elements discussed in this book before the wedding. However, if you are already married, it isn't too late. It will just be a bit more challenging to re-create the honeymoon atmosphere after the newness of marriage has worn off. No matter when you read this book, application of the principles will improve your relationship and hopefully the teachings in this book will provide a basis for many long and productive discussions as you iron out the wrinkles in your marriage.

"If you think you can or you can't, you are right!" so stated a wise, old sage. In other words, you literally become a self-fulfilling prophecy. Given that as a true statement, it is to our advantage to make sure our beginning attitude is what we want. If you are entering into marriage with the idea in the back of your mind that you will divorce if things don't work out, you are sowing the seeds of destruction even before the nuptial knot is tied. As a foundation for your marriage, why not decide that if you are mature enough to get married, you are mature enough to meet and overcome the problems and challenges you are likely to meet?

Once the two of you agree that divorce is not an option when problems arise, then the stage is set to look for other possible solutions to the problems which are common to almost all marriages. When you leave the door open for a possible divorce, so many are tempted to go through that door because it seems to be the easiest solution to the mounting problems you are facing. Even divorce attorneys and marriage counselors are admitting that divorce often creates problems which are more severe than the challenges that precipitated the divorce. Regrettably the experts are coming to believe (usually too late) that it might have been advisable to try a little harder to find agreeable solutions before advocating divorce.

Divorce compounds problems in life. It is like adding the final straw that results in breaking the camel's back. Such a tiny weight but the results are incalculable. If you are already in the unfortunate situation of being divorced, is all lost? Not by any means. It simply means that you will have to try that much harder to take control of those factors which destroyed your previous marriage.

Faultfinding and pointing the finger of accusation at each other, a common problem after divorce, is not only a waste of time but is destructive to the process of problem solving. It really doesn't matter who started the divorce process; the more important issue is to identify and overcome the causing factors so they will not be recur in your next marriage. While it is a statistical reality that divorced people are more likely to divorce a second, third, and fourth time, it doesn't have to be that way. Once the destructive cycles are identified and broken, you stand on the same solid ground as those who have never been divorced.

During the time of dating and becoming more acquainted, give yourselves adequate time to agree upon the basic foundational building blocks of marriage. Jumping into marriage before you really know one another leaves both of you wide open to marriage-shattering surprises after the honeymoon is over. If you really want to get to know each other, avoid putting all of your focus on your physical relationship. Any normal man and any normal woman in the world can successfully engage in sexual intercourse, but it takes a great deal of common ground and mutual determination to be compatible in marriage.

So how do you get to know each other well enough to eliminate the surprises? I would suggest you turn off the television and radio and spend some long hours talking. In fact I call it a "talk-a-thon." This is how it works: You start a statement about something you want to know about your future spouse's attitude. Leave the sentence uncompleted. Your future spouse then completes the sentence, then begins a new sentence that reveals something that he or she wants to know about your attitude. You must honestly complete the sentence. On a very basic level it would go something like:

"My favorite color is—" (he or she would complete the sentence). "The one food I dislike the most is—" (you would complete the sentence). "The optimum number of children in a family is—" (they complete). "The justifiable reasons for going into debt are—" (you complete). You can readily see that within an hour or two you could cover a lot of ground.

Why not just ask the question directly? You could. Many do. But occasionally the questions are misconstrued as confrontational. The statements never are. The only limiting factors are your ability to think through what you want to know and your ability to phrase the statement. If you engage in a "talk-a-thon" several times over a period of time, you will rapidly find that your future mate's attitude becomes almost transparent.

What if you discover some differences? Two options are available: 1) you can call off the marriage if the differences are too big or too many or over really important issues; or 2) you can solve the ones you can agree upon and enter into marriage knowing that you must compromise on other differences. For example, if you want half a dozen children and your future spouse doesn't want any, three is not a compromise. It is too few for you and too many for him or her. You will notice that I didn't suggest as a third option to ignore the differences. Even though you may think that your love is so deep for each other that you can overlook these differences, the time will come in the future when those differences must be addressed. Often when that time arrives you are not in the best of moods and an ugly confrontation results which can weaken your relationship.

If you plan to have a divorce-less marriage, you must not ignore hidden wedges that can weaken the fiber of your marriage in the future. The more honest you both can be and the more issues you can resolve before the marriage, the more likely you are to live in love and harmony after the ceremony and the honeymoon are over.

Having set the stage now for the chapters which follow, let's investigate in a positive way what hidden dangers seem to lurk in the shadows awaiting to devour your dream marriage. I have tried to keep the chapters short and manageable so you won't get bogged down with examples and details. Because this is not written like a storybook, you may read any chapter in any sequence and it should still make sense. In other words, each chapter should stand alone, although you will quickly discover the common threads of communication, compromise, understanding, consideration, tenderness, forgiveness, determination, and genuine love which are woven from the first chapter to the last.

May I wish you success as you take the initiative to improve your marriage and your life. Don't be discouraged because of the difficulty of the challenge. The result of successfully meeting the challenges of marriage is a unity built on love and trust. It is yours for the effort. Marital bliss is not a myth to those who are willing to pay the price. Couples can and do "live happily ever after," but it is not a given. It must be earned. Adjust your attitude, if necessary, to think in terms of successes not failures. Even if you are not perfect (which you won't be!), the end result will be a marriage to be envied by all the doomsday prophets who say that happy marriages are a thing of the past. Prove them wrong as you enjoy the greatest union in the world—a happy marriage.

2

SETTING THE GROUND RULES

— ♥ —

Awhile ago my wife and I were taking our daily walk around the park adjacent to the elementary school in our neighborhood. As we started our first round, a group of boys who appeared to be in about the third or fourth grade were congregating to organize a football game. They were choosing up sides and marking off the goal lines. On our second round of the park they were joyfully playing. On our third round we were surprised to see that they were not playing any more but standing in a circle yelling at each other. We stopped to listen. The leader of one team was accusing the other team of "making up the rules as we go along to favor your team!" The angry response by the leader of the other team quickly led me to conclude that the game was a thing of the past unless they could agree upon the rules. At that point we continued our walk and returned home. The sounds of angry argumentation continued to take precedence over the playing of the game until we were beyond hearing range.

Further pondering the fiasco resulted in seeing a principle which, if ignored, signals tough times in football or in marriage. There needs to be a clearly defined, agreed-upon set of ground rules in order to avoid ugly confrontations during the event. Following is a sampling of the kinds of ground rules which help to avoid marital interruptions.

Rule #1 - **No matter what, we will talk through the problem and find a mutually agreeable solution.** If you agree to this rule, the others become almost automatic. Sometimes family members develop methods of solving problems which leave a lot to be desired. My family had established, fine-tuned, and perfected the art of sulking in order to get their way. My father was a sulker, my grandfather was a sulker, as was my great-grandfather, and so on back to Adam Bott. Each succeeding generation built on the bad habits of the past. Although I don't remember my father well because I was only four-and-a-half years old when he died, others have told me about my his sulking prowess. He would be totally silent for as long as two or three months. Only occasionally would he motion or grunt to indicate what he wanted. On a moment's notice, he would snap out of his sulk and expect everyone to go on as though nothing was wrong. When asked what he was mad at, his most common response was "I can't remember."

How childish and inconsiderate of him. I decided very early in life, that I would never do that to my wife and children. So we agreed to talk things out. My wife only had to say "do you want to talk now or later?" and that was the key phrase we agreed would alert me to my sliding into a sulk. I still have to think twice to make sure I'm not sulking, but our life is so much happier because we agreed to talk.

Rule #2 - **If a conflict arises, or a decision affecting both of us has to be made, we will consult with each other before making a decision.** So often feelings are hurt because one or the other spouse makes a unilateral decision. It often isn't so much what the decision is as that the opinion or consent of the other was not sought. People hate to be ignored or taken for granted. I want my vote to count even if it only confirms the proposition.

It only takes a second to say "let me check with my wife and I'll get right back to you." You can expect some verbal teasing by those who see no value in making a mutual decision. "What's the matter, does your wife make all the decisions for you?" or "Can't you think for yourself? Does your wife hold all the decision-making power in your marriage?" are typical put-downs by people who don't subscribe to the rule. I let them tease. The quality of our relationship is something that even the casual observer readily sees. Sometimes I respond to them and try to share the principle with them, other times I just smile and go off to consult with my wife. Usually the wife of the person taunting is the one who puts the offender in his place. Seldom, ironically, does a woman tease us for wanting to consult. It certainly has kept us from making some dumb decisions and has contributed to the harmony of our marriage.

Violate the principle a few times and watch the normal fallout and you'll see what I mean. Just consider how you would feel if you have no say in matters that affect you. I would suspect it wouldn't take you too long to register a vote of disapproval and set about to rectify the situation.

Rule #3 - **Money matters will be discussed in private and without pressure from outside sources**. Perhaps I can illustrate this principle with an example. We had only been married a couple of weeks when a knock came at our door. We weren't expecting visitors so we were surprised to have a kindly looking older gentleman pay us a visit. He congratulated us on our wedding, talked about our plans, then started laying the groundwork for a sale. He was a life insurance salesman! He was smooth and persuasive. He made me feel like a real heel if I didn't buy a life insurance policy large enough to sustain my wife for the rest of her life in the seemingly unavoidable event that something should happen to me. When he got around to the actual cost, it was about one-third of our total monthly budget. He assured us that he could cut us a special deal if we would sign that very night. We finally got his name and telephone number and told him we'd have to think about it overnight and call him the next day with our decision. Without him there intellectually bullying us, it became apparent that if something happened to me, my young bride could go back and live with her parents until she remarried or got a job to support herself. We didn't have children and so most of his argument was groundless. When I called him the next morning to inform him of our decision, he was very casual as though he expected our negative answer.

We made it a policy never to buy under pressure or over the phone. That decision has saved us a lot of grief over the years. This good man apparently searched through the local newspaper to find who was going to be married. Through whatever means available to him, he found out where they were living and shortly after the honeymoon moved in for the kill.

Other times we have been approached with these "too good to be true" offers which always turned out to be just that— "too good to be true." If you buy yourselves enough time to stand back and consider the offer, you will see that no one is going to give you a million dollars just for sending in a hundred-dollar retainer. They would go broke in a minute at that rate. Whenever you win some fantastic prize for a contest you haven't even entered, you can almost always smell "scam" all over it. Avoid it like a plague or be prepared to learn by sad experience that there really isn't any free lunch.

A twin sister to the "too good to be true" offer is the "it is only good if you sign up right now" ploy. Although all specials designate a time when the sale will end, the salesman who uses that tactic on a regular basis for unsuspecting newlyweds needs a good dose of his own medicine. We had a salesman come to sell us steel siding for our newly-acquired house. We had budgeted closely to get into the house. He said that if we signed on the line that very night, he could get us a deal that would immediately double or even triple the value of our house. The bottom line was that it would have cost almost as much as the house did. There would have been absolutely no way for us to make both the house payment and the siding payment. It would have resulted in almost immediate bankruptcy. The salesman was relentless and finally we had to physically usher him out of our house. When he was gone, we looked at each other and started to laugh. Thankfully our rule had saved our bacon again.

Rule #4 - **Any one or any thing that tries to divide us or pit us against each other is to be held in mutual distrust**. We really believe that marriage is to be an arrangement where the man leaves his father and his mother and cleaves unto his wife and none else (see Genesis 2:24). Sometimes (either in fun or maliciously) your friends may try to throw a wrench in the gears which cause your marriage to work. If it is truly in fun it is tasteless humor. If it is malicious they join with so many others who seem bent on destroying anything that is good. In either event, you need to be watchful lest they blindside you with their tactics.

We had only been married a few months when a mutual acquaintance of my wife and me met me on the campus of the university I was attending and innocently (not!) asked me if I was sure I knew where my wife was and was I sure she was home alone? I reassured her that I was sure she was home alone and there was nothing to worry about. She just remarked over her shoulder as she left, "I just thought you would want to be sure!" A nasty innuendo. Nothing overt or concrete to accuse her of, just a suggestion of unfaithfulness.

That evening at the dinner table, I mentioned the rather strange exchange with our friend. To my surprise, my new wife said, "That is strange. I met the same friend earlier in the day. She innocently asked who the cute young girl my husband was with on campus?" As we began to compare notes, it was apparent that this "friend," for reasons known only to herself, wanted to set us at odds with each other. My wife had assured the friend that I studied with several different girls and that she was perfectly sure I wasn't cheating on her. The "friend" had responded, "Well, I just didn't want you to get hurt!" Innocent? We didn't think so. Although we continued to associate with her, we were never quite as unguarded around her. It was a good lesson for us both. Even an innocent rattlesnake bite is poisonous. Watch out for the snakes!

The second half of the rule is also important. Any one or any thing that tries to pit us against each other is to be viewed with caution. Certain movements which have gained popularity in recent years try to pit husband and wife against each other as though they were competitors. We have found it non-unifying and very destructive to compare pay checks, compare and contrast talents, or in any other way to compete. We are a team and as in so many other things the united strength of our team far exceeds the combination of our individual strengths. As we have grown together into a single unit, we have identified which member of the team has talents in certain areas and capitalized on those strengths. For example, my wife is very creative and artistic. If you are familiar with the Herrman Brain Dominance scale—she is a "limbic right brain." On the other hand, I am a "cerebral left brain." Totally opposite from her, I am analytical, exact, mathematical, etc. Because my strength is where it is, I balance the checkbook. My wife could, if she really tried, balance the checkbook, but it would probably be wrong. That just isn't her talent. On the other hand, she has difficulty understanding why I can't draw a picture. She claims that anyone can draw. I can't. So whenever there is something artistic or creative to do, she takes the lead. I don't know how I would function without her. She says the same thing of me.

Rule #5 - **Keeping each other informed is of paramount importance**. It seems to be the lot of the newly married to worry excessively over the safety of their mate. If the husband is half an hour late for dinner, surely he is laying mortally wounded on some highway. If the wife stays half an hour too long at the department store, surely she had been kidnaped and is presently being tortured and abused. What a relief that those scenarios seldom happen. A courtesy telephone call could set troubled minds at ease with little or no expense. The reason I list this as a ground rule is probably because I have broken it so often. I am now looking from the vantage point of thirty years of experience and saying I should have been more considerate. It seems that I have become the worrier in later years. Now, with the shoe on the other foot, I find I don't like to be kept in the dark as to my wife's whereabouts. So we try to call if we are going to be late.

As the family has matured and everyone is going in their own direction, we have found it not only helpful but absolutely necessary to sit down in the morning and outline our daily plans. It only takes a minute but it is invaluable in arranging cars, rides, meals, meetings, etc. Since we have done this for years, the children have grown up being required to plan far enough in advance to avoid adversely impacting the family with their failure to keep us informed. In fact, if the plan does not get discussed in the morning exchange, the answer is "no" when permission is sought later in the day. Although that isn't an ironclad rule, it has greatly reduced the number of surprises when parties and activities are sprung on us without warning.

When the other members of our family hear what everyone else has going, very often they willingly offer to forego some party in order to provide babysitting for the ones staying at home. It is so much fun to have all these people as advocates rather than adversaries. Start early in your marriage showing the courtesy to your mate by keeping them informed of your plans and whereabouts.

Rule #6 - **Raised voices and physical violence will never be used to make your point or get your way**. In a world seemingly bent on self-destruction, we need more soft voices and gentle hands. Abuse is an ugly word and has no place in marriage. Agree before you are married that solving problems by shouting at each other or physically attacking each other is not an option. It is so easy to say the words in formulating this rule. It will require maturity to test the very best in order to implement it. But it can be done if you both are determined to make it work.

In a fit of rage, we often speak words which leave scars even when forgiveness has been sought. Memories of being beat up by or beating up someone you love are difficult visions to erase from your mind. I can't put into words how satisfying it is to look back on nearly three decades of marriage without regretting how I have talked to my wife or how I have treated her. As I mentioned in the introduction, we disagree all the time but not by using childish tactics. In a later chapter I'll discuss in detail the "how to's" of disagreeing without being disagreeable.

It will be sufficient for this chapter to merely say that if you think you cannot live together without verbally and physically abusing each other, you are totally right. If you honestly believe you can live together in a marriage without physical or verbal abuse, you have a good chance of making it become a reality. Your attitude and mutual decision will make the difference.

Unfortunately, it would be too easy for this chapter to evolve into an entire book because almost everything we will talk of in subsequent chapters is a basic ground rule. However, these six basic rules may give you the idea of the kinds of things that are foundational and essential to a happy marriage. As you discuss with your mate these items, others will surely come to mind: putting our family first before the extended family or friends; never saying anything negative about each other to friends and relatives; solving problems in privacy rather than before others but also allowing your children to watch you model problem solving; making frequent mid-course corrections when either or both of you feel your marriage is getting off course. Add your own basic rules and then resolve to live by them.

If you find that one or more of your rules are unrealistic or just plain wrong (i.e. it causes more harm than it does good), don't be afraid to change them. When I was young and single I was an expert on marriage and child rearing. Then I got married and was content to be an expert on child rearing. Then our children came along and I realized that I was just like everyone else—learning the lessons of life one day at a time. Some of the rules we had when we were first married seem sort of silly now. We thought they sounded pretty good, but they just didn't work. This entire book is the result of many mid-course corrections. Probably if I were to write it ten years from now, I would modify some of the counsel to be given in this book. However, having proven the counsel over the past thirty years, I have confidence that not too many major changes will be necessary.

Don't ignore the opportunity to sit down and dream and plan and decide together how you will insure happiness and success in your marriage. To fail to plan is to plan to fail, although a common cliche, it is also true.

3

AVOIDING BAD HABITS

— ♥ —

Wise King Solomon said: "Where there is no vision, the people perish" (Proverbs 29:18). Said another way, if you don't have an idea of what an ideal marriage is like, how will you know whether you are progressing towards it or not? "Bad" is a comparative term. Bad compared to what? In this chapter we will discuss choosing an ideal or model and then how to avoid taking avoidable detours in your journey to become the ideal.

Is there such a thing as a perfect couple? Probably not here on earth. There are those who live their married lives in love and harmony, who enjoy doing things together, who seem empty and alone when they are separated, and a host of other descriptors. But not everyone would like a marriage like that. So it is up to the two of you to decide on what a perfect couple is like.

The easiest way to decide is to look around and find one or more older couples who seem to have that special something in their relationship that the two of you want in yours. Perhaps you will find exactly what you want in a favorite grandpa and grandma. It may be that you have to build a composite couple composed of the best from several couples. You may have to envision a fictitious couple in your minds because a true role model cannot be found. You may want to fantasize and dream of a heavenly couple and what they would be like. Whatever method you employ to find that perfect couple, you need to have them well defined. If you can't find or envision them at first, take the best shot you can and then add to the vision as your experience in marriage gives you a broader perspective.

The couple my wife and I adopted as role models were very old when we saw a television reporter interview them for their 65th wedding anniversary. In spite of their both being wheelchair-bound, they were sharp intellectually and very quick-witted. It might be instructive to summarize the interview. The reporter had quite obviously had an argument with his wife before going on this assignment. After the opening amenities, his first question to the couple was something like, "Well, Mr. and Mrs. Smith, you purportedly have the perfect marriage. How often do you fight with each other?" With the camera trained on Mr. Smith, he responded: "Why young man, we have never fought with each other!" One may as well have thrown a bucket of ice water in the young reporter's face. He was caught off guard. In almost a whining, pleading voice he asked: "How have you lived together for 65 years and avoided fighting?" Mr. Smith turned to his wife and said, "Sweetheart, why don't you answer that question?" She said, "I will. We just decided before we got married that we would never get angry at the same time." By this time the reporter had regained some composure. He retorted, "Well, what if you do get angry at the same time?" Mrs. Smith turned to Mr. Smith and said, "Dear, why don't you answer that one?" Mr. Smith replied, "I would be glad to. Young man, we decided that if we both got angry at the same time, that I would go for a walk until we could both cool off and get the issue back in proper perspective." Then he added, "And young man, I've spent a lot of nights out walking!"

Laughter broke the tension and the rest of the interview was folksy and down-to-earth wisdom which enriched the lives of all who would listen and apply their counsel. The interview happened six months before we were scheduled to be married. We looked at each other and readily agreed that they had what we wanted. We had our role model.

Having grown up all of my conscious life without a father in the home, I have become a natural people watcher. Perhaps the death of my father was one of the greatest blessings in my life. I could not rely solely upon the home example because I didn't have one. As a result I watched every husband and wife relationship I could observe making two mental lists: (1) things I want to have in my marriage, and (2) things I want to avoid in my marriage.

You will need to be serious about building a role model. You can, without being accusatory, look at the failures of your own parents. Learn from their mistakes. You would not be very honest if you failed to note the successes they have also enjoyed. No marriages that are totally negative stay together over an extended period of time.

As you identify qualities or attributes you want, make sure you discuss them as a couple. If one of you ascribes to a certain philosophy or characteristic and the other one does not, you are creating an environment for possible conflicts. Be very careful in the ideal you decide upon; if you successfully become that couple, countless others will use you as their role model. Just as Mr. and Mrs. Smith had no idea of how powerful an impact they had on our lives, so you will never know how many people will be looking to you two as their heroes. The impact will not be limited to your children and future grandchildren, but may include neighborhood orphans or those without fathers or mothers in the home (like I was), or young couples approaching marriage, or already-established couples attempting to make course corrections.

Many couples fall short of being ideal because of bad habits that have crept into their marriages. Although an exhaustive list is not feasible, let's at least investigate a few "bad habits" which will act as examples of things to avoid if you want to build a divorce-less marriage.

Don't cut each other down (even in jest). I have been counseling couples for longer than we've been married. I seem to attract those with problems. As I have listened to their recitals, there seems to be a common thread. They start off joking with each other, an innocent matching of wits. As the session progresses, one or the other questions to himself/herself whether the jesting comment was intended as a cut or just a verbal put-down. Just to insure they are covered, they send out a cut with a barb on it to counter the alleged cut they just received. Now the other partner perceives that the last cut was not innocent. The barb ripped a little flesh. Not to be out-done, the next verbal volley includes a bigger barb. From here on feelings are hurt, flesh is flying, and relationships are weakened. What started in fun, ended in an ugly fight.

How do you overcome the tendency to "get even?" There are two ways we have found to be effective. The first is a simple question, the second is a controlled tactic. When you perceive that a verbal slam has been thrown your way, simply say, "That comment really hurt my feelings. Did you intend to cut me down?" If your commitment to each other is genuine and deep, the offending partner will have just a split second to reconsider the comment. Instantaneous repentance, a rephrasing of the comment, and an apology will avoid further hurt. "I'm sorry. I didn't mean to hurt your feelings. This is what I meant to (or should have) say," then make it right. In those early days of our marriage, I was forever putting my foot in my mouth and having to admit I didn't mean what I said. Thankfully my young bride was patient and eventually we learned together to be more accurate and precise in what we said. Accuracy is hitting the right target, precision is hitting exactly what you aim at. You can be perfectly precise and hit the wrong target.

The second way is to avoid playing verbal tennis. How would you react if you were playing tennis with a person and they never returned your volley? After awhile, you would tire of the game and move on to something more challenging. If your spouse serves a verbal cut over your net, you are not obliged to return it. Let it go. Over the years in working and counseling with both adults and teenagers, it seems to be a difficult thing to get them to realize they do not have to return the verbal volley. It is mostly an ego thing. "No one is going to say that to me and get away with it!" is a typical response. My question is, "Why not?" As they sputter for an answer, I usually continue, "You don't have to prove yourself to anyone or to defend yourself from unjust attacks. Just let it go and before long the offender will tire of the childish game and either move on or redirect the conversation to a more acceptable topic."

Reports that have come back over the years have proven that avoiding verbal tennis is a viable way of defusing otherwise explosive situations. It puts you in control; rather than being a reactionary, you choose how you will act. The feelings of power and control are well worth resisting the urge to "get even."

Don't use undesirable control tactics against each other. That urge to "get even" is powerful after the honeymoon is over. If you succumb to the urge, you will find many areas in which depriving one another can be used as control tactics. Although available, these should not be used. The most obvious example is sex. If sex is used as a "reward for being good and a punishment for being bad," you begin to develop an adversarial relationship. "Why should I meet his needs" said one wife, "when he ignores my needs?" The question is valid, the method of coercing him to meet her needs may backfire in a big way. A hot-headed response from the offended husband in that case was, "Well, she needn't think she is the only source of sex available to me!" From that critical juncture either a drastic change in tactics will be employed or destruction of the marriage is eminent.

Not fixing his favorite meal because he forgot your birthday may punish the offending husband but it does nothing to rectify the mistake or strengthen the relationship. A more desirable method might be to give ample hints the week before your birthday or an even more sure method would be to tell him directly that next Tuesday is your birthday. Because I'm a person who has to have a thousand things going all at once, my wife has avoided hurt feelings by telling me what her needs are and how I can meet them.

Although it drives the kids crazy, we agreed that when I get so involved in my professional life that I fail to meet her needs, she will stand blocking the hallway to our bedroom and say, "Kiss me, you fool!" I immediately respond by sweeping her off her feet and giving her a passionate kiss. The kids roll their eyes and make comments of incredulity but they know I love and respect their mother and that we are still happily married.

Failing to do the wash because your husband didn't take out the garbage not only results in dirty clothes and overflowing trash cans but also a strained marital relationship. Refusing to pass on telephone messages because your spouse opened the mail addressed to you can only result in hurt feelings and increasingly hostile feelings between you. They are bad habits which need to be avoided or changed before your relationship can improve. You can see that there is a multitude of like adversarial situations where you use unfair tactics in retaliation for some oversight or wrong leveled against you.

Part of avoiding these kinds of bad habits is being honest enough with yourself and your future mate to realize what undesirable control tactics you each have used over the years. Being aware of them and resolving not to use them is usually the first giant step towards solving the problems before they become an issue.

I haven't met anyone who likes to be controlled or manipulated or put into a situation where they feel they have no other options but to conform. It requires a lot of work and a lot of patience in figuring out how to persuade a person to change or conform without using force. In spite of the difficulty of the task, the long term benefits so far outweigh the immediate, short term gains of coercion that they are hardly on the same scale.

Don't take each other for granted. The courting process is an interesting one. The guy may hover over his girlfriend as though she were the singular most important person on the globe. Flowers, candy, cards, courtesies, manners, etc. are all ways of winning her hand. Girls may primp, cook, participate in activities foreign to them, make sure the scent of perfume is always evident, send "gushy" love letters, put notes in school books and lunches, etc. all to gain approval of her man.

After the honeymoon when life begins to become more routine, it is easy to forget to do the things which bought your spouse's favor before the marriage. When you begin to take for granted that your spouse will always be there and always perform the expected duties just because they did once, it tends to send the silent message that you aren't valued as you were before.

Earlier in the chapter I mentioned Mr. and Mrs. Smith and their ideal marriage. He had established a habit before they were married of standing whenever she entered the room. It was a mark of respect that never went unnoticed and never grew old. That may not be a practice you care to establish, but it worked for them.

Such a simple thing as "thank you" or "please" can convey your appreciation and let your spouse know you recognize the sacrifices he or she is making for you. An occasional "love letter" just reminding them how fortunate you are to have chosen them as your mate and how much deeper your love for them is now you've been married a few years does wonders for a relationship.

Life has a way of demanding more time than is available. We live in the fast track and so it is easy to ignore our spouse because they don't demand daily attention. What a terrible mistake. Long after retirement, after the children are reared and have left home, after "things" have lost their appeal and (hopefully) money is no longer a high priority, you will still have each other. If you have ignored each other to give attention to the more demanding items (kids, work, etc.) you may discover that there isn't enough of a relationship between you to retire to! How sad to see people who have been married forty or fifty years getting divorced because they are two strangers living under the same roof. That doesn't have to happen if you refuse to take each other for granted.

As with each of the chapters, there is only room for a sampling or a limited number of examples to illustrate the concepts. Perhaps these few examples will suffice. Now you have the opportunity to take a long walk and decide between you the potential pitfall which seem to have tripped up so many marriages of your families and friends. Unfortunately, the world provides many examples of what not to do.

You may want to spend some time with friends or relatives who have divorced. Let them talk through the problems leading up to the separation. Without asking them to justify themselves, they will reveal thought patterns and problem-solving procedures which will be obviously flawed from your perspective. Few people are willing to shoulder the blame for problems—especially failure in something as important as marriage. As the people you are talking to blame the other party or point out where they went wrong, make a mental list. See if there is a principle with even broader application that you can apply to help avoid a similar fate in your marriage.

Now that you have gleaned what information you can from those who have failed, take at least an equal amount of time (probably considerably more) to talk with couples who seem to be making a success of their marriage. Ask them point blank what they are doing to insure happiness and stability in their marriage. Don't be surprised if it takes them awhile to come up with the answers. Many couples are unaware of what they do that contributes to the success of their relationship. If you press them a little, they will start to identify things they do—which they assume everyone does—that makes them love each other more deeply as time passes.

Don't be surprised if the two lists (the don't's from the divorced and the do's from the happily married) look like opposites on a continuum. In fact they will be. For example the divorced may say, "My spouse never listened to me" while the happily married may say, "We spend a lot of time talking to each other." Along the continuum between the two extremes will be the rest of your acquaintances. To the degree we communicate we are happy. To the degree we fail to communicate we are sad. Every one of the factors from both lists will find themselves on the continuum from "never" to "always." Be wise enough to recognize the pitfalls and avoid them.

4

"I Know What You're Thinking"

— ♥ —

As you spend more time together during the courtship part of your relationship, you will discover that you can begin to anticipate what your fiancé is thinking or what he or she will do or say next. It is almost uncanny. It is sort of fun. A silent glance between the two of you can communicate more than an entire dialogue. After you are married, this "talent" seems to expand even more. This is sort of a mixed blessing—part good and part potentially destructive.

There are many times when silent communication will be necessary as decisions have to be made when it is not convenient to take a break and talk things over. If you have refined the talent of silent communication, it can enhance your ability to make mutual decisions even when private conversation is not possible. That is good.

You may want to devise a system of "signals" to help in your communication to insure that you are not misinterpreting the signal. We have a couple of signals which are not obvious to others but helpful to us. If I agree or vote "yes" on a proposal, I scratch my head with my right hand. If I disagree or vote "no", I use the left hand. It is so simple but usually not obvious. Let me illustrate. I am a teacher and it is not unusual for me to have 250 adults in a seminar. I feel confident enough to allow them to ask whatever questions they want concerning the topic of discussion. Over the years one gets the impressions that he has heard all the questions there are in a given area. Occasionally a seminar attendee will ask a question which I have never considered before. Then the pressure is on. To be able to respond in front of a group that large sometimes causes stress of the first magnitude. You probably can identify by your own experience how much more difficult it is to reason and think clearly when you are under pressure. When my wife is in the seminar (which she frequently is), I look to her for some help. It wouldn't be appropriate to stop and discuss with her the answer. Without her being under the direct pressure of having to respond, she can signal her opinion without being noticed at all. She is often a life saver.

You can probably anticipate already the down side of silent communication. It is subject to misinterpretation. Let's say that over the years you become so proficient that you can "read" your partner's mind correctly ninety percent of the time. What destroys marriages? Right, the other ten percent!

So how can you use the silent communication to your advantage and avoid the problems which invariably result from misreading your partner's body language? It isn't that difficult. By establishing several signals, you can register your vote or send your message without worrying about being misunderstood. I noticed a colleague touch his little finger and thumb together when his wife dropped him off at school. I asked him about it. He said that was their signal which meant "I love you, see you next round." Probably no one else noticed and perhaps no one else cared. Between the two of them it was a gesture of continuing the courtship.

The way to avoid misinterpreting silent messages is to ask! If you or your spouse sense that something is wrong between you or that one or the other has sent a message intended to offend or hurt, agree not to take offense until you have asked. "What you said really hurt my feelings. Did you intend to hurt me?" Just a simple question like that can defuse some potentially explosive situations.

Even if the cut or jab was intended to hurt, the asking of the question by the offended spouse gives the offender just a split second to reconsider and change his or her vote. I call that "rapid repentance." Because we are human, we still make a lot of mistakes. So when I say something offensive and my wife asks if I intended to hurt her feelings, I quickly repent and rephrase the statement without the barb. She is no dummy. She knows I was in the wrong. But, because we are really trying to make a heaven on earth with our marriage, she allows me a second chance to say what I intended without offense.

I really don't know what would happen if I were so angry or meanspirited that I restated the original cut with the barb. Thankfully, because of the ground rules we set before we were married, I have never tried a second offense to see what would happen. If I am in a bad mood and know that I will just make things worse by continuing the conversation, we have agreed to take a "time-out" like in athletics. We even use the time out signal to buy some time where we can both stand back and reevaluate what we are doing and saying and then approach the solution with more self-control. Although we use the "time-out" signal very infrequently, it is there as a safety valve to help us avoid saying things that will weaken our relationship.

There is another potentially dangerous flaw in believing that you know what your mate is thinking. It is the dreaded disease of "Silence." Before marriage, you were probably like most other young people. You may have chattered for hours with each other talking about anything and everything under the sun. Even during the honeymoon and those first few months of marriage, couples seem to have so much to talk about. As the newness of marriage wears off, there is a tendency to talk less and less.

In the hundreds of couples I have counseled with over the years who have had the silence problem, they almost universally agree that it started when they decided they knew each other so well that verbal communication was not necessary. What started as a source of pride, being able to tell what their mate was thinking without actually asking, became a wedge that was driven between partners and weakened the relationship.

Perhaps being conscious of the pitfall of silence is sufficient to help you avoid the problem. In our marriage we have adopted the policy, "if you want to know what I am thinking, there is only one failsafe way—ask me!" It has proven priceless over the years. Hurt feelings have been avoided or quickly mended, misunderstandings have been quickly resolved, relationship weakening comments have been eliminated or greatly reduced, and our marriage is stronger because of what we decided to do.

It seems almost impossible that the two of you would ever have trouble talking. A quick analysis of your situation will probably reveal that during the courtship stage your conversations were relatively stress free. It is easy to talk about issues which do not have such a potentially explosive impact on you personally. World problems are still far away and usually affect other people. Even state and local issues, even though they are closer to you, are still "other people's problems." In marriage all of that changes. Now the conversations are more serious and more personal. It seems like virtually every issue directly impacts both of you. Since marriage is a constant state of changing and adapting to accommodate your spouse, everything has a price tag.

Ignoring problems is not a good idea. Seldom do problems solve themselves. Because communication is so vital to the solution of problems, failure to keep the lines of communication open causes almost immediate problems. When decisions are made based on your assumption that you know what your mate is thinking, the problems are only compounded.

There is yet another twist to the "I know what you are thinking paradigm," it is "You think that . . . ." Telling another person (even your mate!) what they are thinking or feeling is the epitome of presumptuousness. Some of the most childish arguments couples have had in my presence have been when they are standing toe-to-toe and telling each other what the other one is thinking and feeling. I usually listen in horrified amusement for a little while then say, "Wouldn't it be more productive if you stopped telling each other what the other thinks or feels and express your own thoughts and feelings?" Once they realize what they are doing, it becomes obvious to them that no one is in a position to expound on what someone else is thinking. It is almost like mud slinging in politics. Each candidate seems to major in informing the public about what the other candidate is thinking or intending. It would be refreshing in politics as well as in marriage to have each party clearly lay out their own agenda.

In mediating one particularly ugly marital battle where the partners were "confessing each other's sins," I physically stood between them and acted as a go-between. "Your spouse said you think that..., is that correct?" "No, that isn't what I think at all." After going back and forth for a few volleys, it became apparent to both of them that it would be much more productive to calm down and tell what they were thinking and feeling. As they began to listen to each other, they were both surprised that they weren't that far apart on their points of view. The differences were not as many and as huge as they originally thought. Thankfully that couple had a very successful conclusion to our counseling sessions. Unfortunately, not all couples will allow the spouse to speak for themselves. More serious trouble is always the result.

It does little or no good to stand back and point the finger of blame at your spouse for failing to communicate. That only results in a shouting match. If you are determined to find solutions to your challenges, it is much more effective to sit down and lay the issues out before you and talk them through. At first there may seem to be some silent resistance to talking about the problems. As you persevere you will find it less difficult. Before long you both will begin to anticipate your problem solving sessions because it puts you back on the same team and makes life flow more freely. Refusing to re-open the communication lines only postpones the inevitable and magnifies the problems associated with getting back on the right course. Permanently refusing to talk through the problems will result in either two strangers living under the same roof or the ultimate break-up of your marriage.

Based on my experience in dealing with silence, I would vote to eliminate altogether the idea of reading one another's mind. Although there are some fun and productive results, the potential for failure so far outweighs the possible good that it isn't worth taking the chance. The marriage that we are discussing is a 100% marriage. Since couples correctly "know what my spouse is thinking" only ninety percent of the time, it seems like a good idea to approach with extreme caution the idea of mind reading. Consider the benefits and the potential costs and decide for yourselves.

5

PROBLEMS: STUMBLING BLOCKS OR STEPPING STONES?

— ♥ —

During the early days of television, I remember seeing several movie series where everyone always enjoyed a blissful marriage. Often the hero and heroine would ride romantically into the sunset, leaving the impression that the remainder of their lives would be one blissful romantic episode after another. The older I got the more real ugliness in marriage I observed. Some of my friends' parents divorced, sad cases of child abuse surfaced, hostility in marriage and families were revealed. Then I began to wonder if anyone was "living happily ever after."

The older I became the more questions I started asking myself and others. "Is marriage supposed to be a state of blissful serenity?" "Is it healthy to have arguments in marriage and between family members?" "Is it possible to live together without friction and hard feelings?" The more questions I asked, the more apparent it became that the attitude of the couples made more difference than what they were going through. If they viewed problems as negative and something to be avoided at all costs, then they were often frustrated when problems arose.

When couples view problems as inevitable, non-threatening elements of a marriage, they are less likely to see them as potentially marriage threatening. Since you are bringing two separate view points into your marriage, wouldn't it be worthwhile to investigate how your spouse views problems? In watching everyone from the royalty of England to the glamorous stars in Hollywood to the couple down the street, it is immediately obvious that everyone has problems to face.

Perhaps it isn't so much "what" we go through as "how" we cope with the problems that makes the difference. Some couples seem to be challenged by financial matters. Other couples struggle with "in-law problems." Still other couples are stressed to the point of breaking by "children problems." No matter which area or areas you are blessed (?) to have problems in, they need not be marriage threatening if you tackle them head on.

Over the years as I have worked with couples at risk, it has become apparent that those who expected that they would be different in that they would never have any problems, were often the ones who were stressed when problems arose. Those who were mature enough to realize that welding two individuals and two families together would produce some challenges, were less likely to misinterpret their problems as marriage threatening.

Many couples report an experience similar to this: "I woke up one morning and looked at the ceiling and thought to myself, 'I have married the wrong person.'" At that critical juncture the marriage either takes a path leading to solidarity, depth, and beauty or it heads towards disaster. What does an experience like that mean? Nothing, only that the honeymoon is over! Now that the newness of the physical relationship is over, a couple needs to focus on building a broader foundation.

If you don't realize what is happening to you and that almost everyone goes through something like it, you may think you've made a real, terrible mistake. Granting that you are no different than the rest of humanity, what do you do? Start taking the initiative to strengthen your social relationship, your intellectual relationship, your spiritual relationship, and your physical (non-sexual) relationship. As you do,

34

you will find that what you thought was "love" before marriage was not nearly as deep and beautiful as what you are experiencing now.

Part of the genius of really growing into love (not falling in love as the movies portray) is going through hard times together. Think back to your youth. What made certain people your special friends? Wasn't it that you shared common experiences, some of which were extremely difficult? Boy Scout camp-outs, girl scout outings, school projects, participation on an athletic team, in the band, in a club, etc. Those are the friendship-building experiences. Just going to school with someone wasn't really a bonding experience as is evident from the fact that (unless you come from a very small school) you were not really close to a lot of your school mates.

If that is what made you close as friends, why wouldn't that work in marriage? In fact, it does. If you didn't marry your very best friend, you can change that as you "suffer" through things together. I'm not at all suggesting that you get a divorce and marry your best friend. I am saying that by experiencing the challenges incident to life, you will soon find that you have a new "best" friend—your spouse.

It wouldn't be wise to go out looking for problems. Life seems so designed that the problems come looking for you. As you are faced with the normal catastrophes of life, it is productive to look at each other, smile, roll up your sleeves, and start solving and over-coming the problem.

Before going too far, it is essential to analyze the cause of the problem. If you have brought it on yourselves because of poor planning or unwise choices, resolve to correct the problem early. If the money runs out by the tenth of the month and you still have twenty days to go before the next pay check, sit down immediately and see where the holes are in your budget. Then patch them. It may very well require some serious self-control to avoid making that kind of a blunder again. If you don't learn, you will very likely repeat the problem in following months.

I started with an example in finances because the major stressor in marriage is financial irresponsibility. A future chapter will be devoted to some sound principles for money management. For right now, we'll just mention finances as a potential problem area. Running short of money is not something that cannot be remedied. Not being willing to admit you have a problem and then devising an acceptable solution to the problem is a major issue.

If poor choices or decisions have resulted in the problems mounting, that is rather easy to solve. Just identify the problem and fix it. If the problems are not the result of conditions or circumstances within your control, you will need to take a different approach.

If someone totals your car while you are parked at the grocery store and then drives off without leaving a name or address, you have no control over that. Rather than falling to pieces or getting angry with each other for "parking in the wrong place," why not take a more rational approach. After all, it is impossible to "unwreck" your car! So look at your options and select the one that is least painful given the situation you are in without getting ugly with each other. You can rest assured that if your spouse knew the car would be damaged, he or she would have parked some other place.

There are times when you really are the source of your problems but the connection may not be so obvious. Taking too many credit hours at school, working too many hours, volunteering for too many committee assignments, trying to help out too many neighbors can all contribute to stress in your marriage. Too much of a good thing is not a good thing. If your health fails because you're not taking time to eat and sleep, the sickness might be avoided by using some common sense and learning to say "no." Be totally honest with yourself. Stand back and evaluate where you are using your resources whether financial, or emotional, or physical (including time). If you can adjust one or more areas to reduce the demands, you may well avert problems in your marriage.

If you cannot control the problems and they are not caused by you, learn to take them in stride. Six months after we were married, my new wife had to have an emergency appendectomy. It would have been easy to shift the blame to my in-laws who should have had her recurring side pains diagnosed and treated before we got married. They didn't, so what good would it do to get angry with them? It caused us to grow even closer as we figured out how we could pay for this unexpected emergency. We could have been bitter but that would only have made the situation worse. As it turned out, it was one of the early solidifying events of our marriage which has paid big dividends over the years.

If the problems are too big and come in multiple doses to the point you cannot cope with them, get some help. Usually a clergyman or a wise relative or your parents may be able to give counsel and direction and maybe even some financial help. All of us who are older have empathy for those of you who are just starting out. It was only a few years ago when we were suffering through those difficult first years as newlyweds. Usually an older person can help you prioritize your problems and give direction on how to handle them. They may even be willing to contact your debtors and negotiate an extension on your payments and possibly a reduction on the interest you have to pay. Riding the earth around the sun a few dozen times more than you have, the older people often know the ropes better than you do and how to make things happen. Don't feel like a failure when you need to ask for assistance.

I have known couples who seemed to be "blessed" with so many problems during the first year of marriage that I thought it impossible for them to survive. But survive they did and even prospered under those trying circumstances. Other couples were crushed by fewer and less intense problems as the first couple. If it isn't the number and weight of the problems that makes the difference, what is it? It is the attitude with which you meet the problems that really signals either success or defeat. Decide even before you are married that you will make a game out of solving problems.

We have in our marriage a time called the "laugh time." It is when everything seems to be going wrong and we wonder if anything else can happen. Sometimes there isn't anything you can do but throw your head back and give a big belly laugh. Nothing has changed but the problems don't seem quite so insurmountable. If you allow the problems to depress you and put you into a mental condition near panic, it will greatly reduce your creativity in solving the problems.

Two friends were really under fire with mounting problems in their marriage. We were concerned about them to the point we decided to drive to their apartment and make sure they were all right. When we arrived we found a note on the door which read "Gone Fishin,' we'll be back Saturday evening. Sorry we missed you. Please call back!" At first I thought, "How could they just walk away from all their problems like that?" Then I realized that camping and fishing didn't cost any more than staying at home and worrying. When they got home on Saturday night, they were rested and relaxed and had taken the time to get a new outlook on their problems. Before long they were back on top and everything worked out fine.

When the problems become so large that there seems to be no way out, take a break. Most of the problems will still be there when you come back from a mini-vacation. Sleep on the problems and try solving them in the morning when you are both mentally fresh and physically renewed. Many problems have solutions which are obvious in the morning that evaded your efforts to find them late at night. I am not suggesting that you postpone indefinitely the solution of your problems. Face them at a reasonable pace and at a level not to exceed your mental and physical capabilities.

We have taken a leaf out of their book of solutions and gone to our cabin occasionally to get a "new fix" on life. On a regular basis we go for a ride, a hike, a camp-out or take a hike down by the lake to just get a change of scenery. Not infrequently we will meet someone at our place of retreat who is also experiencing the problems of life. Talking over our situation with our new friends often results in new, fresh ideas. Sometimes just listening to the challenges others are facing puts a new light on our problems. Seldom do we come away from a sharing session by wishing we could exchange our problems for theirs.

Prioritizing and recognizing which problems can be handled and which ones cannot helps ease the tension. Take the big, demanding problems first—those which cannot be ignored or postponed. After rank-ordering your list, identify those over which you have no control. Develop the skill of not letting them bother you. A young lady came in for some counseling a while ago. She was at her wits' end. Her widowed mother was due for surgery the following week, her brother had been busted for selling illegal drugs, plus he had gotten his fourteen-year-old girlfriend pregnant. Her sixteen-year-old sister was pregnant and her boyfriend had just skipped town. The girl talking with me was failing out of school and was in danger of losing her job.

I thought she was going to collapse in my office. After calming her down, we took a paper and rank-ordered the problems. Mom's operation was at the top. Then I asked her some questions which confirmed in her mind how "out of it" I was. I asked, "Did you get your sister pregnant?" She said "of course not!" "Can you get her un-pregnant?" "No." "Then let's not deal with that one right now." The same line of reasoning was used on her brother's problems. She rightly realized that she was not the one who was busted for selling drugs and that she couldn't get him released from jail and she really couldn't do anything about his girlfriend's pregnancy. As we talked about each problem and made a list of things she could do, her anxiety level dropped. Before the hour was up, she was laughing and back to her bubbly self. Nothing had changed! Every problem she came in to my office with was still there. The only thing that had changed was her attitude towards the problems. A fresh new perspective had made insurmountable problems very manageable.

There is no question that she could have mentally collapsed. What good would that have done? She seemed to be the only person in the dysfunctional family who was thinking right. Her problems became the source of helping her grow and mature. Will she have clear sailing from here on because she handled all of her problems? Probably not. But she will be better equipped next time to meet the problems even when they come in waves. Problems are neither good or bad. Life is neither good or bad. It all depends on your attitude towards what happens to you. What a thrill you'll both get when you resolutely determine that you are going to face and overcome every problem you encounter.

This is not intended to be a comprehensive list of "how to cope with problems." Part of the growing experiences of life come from knowing that problems can be overcome and then combining your talents as husband and wife to master the problems. Good luck in your quest. It doesn't seem to be an option to avoid problems altogether, so why not make the best of them?

6

ATTACKING THE PROBLEM AND NOT YOUR MATE

— ❤ —

On the television, in magazines, on radio talk shows, and in newspapers, the reports multiply *ad nauseam* about physical, mental, sexual, and psychological abuse within families. What started out as a hoped-for perfect marriage somehow deteriorated into a battlefield, a nightmare, a living hell. Unfortunately, too many good marriages are falling casualty to the abuse disease. It is my contention that no couples begin their marriage with the idea of abusing or being abused by their mate. Nothing "just happens!" When we fail to adequately prepare for the difficulties inherent in marriage, we set ourselves up for failure.

One of the more difficult tasks to master is to separate the problem from the person who either causes or is associated with the problem. For example, later in life as the children begin to mature, it is not easy to love the child when his or her behavior is detestable. It is not easy but it is possible if you have perfected the skill during the early years of marriage.

Probably the major "killer" of rationally solving problems is anger. When a person reacts out of rage or excessive anger, common sense and the ability to reason seem to be jettisoned along the way. Therefore, the first resolve needs to be to stand back from the situation and get control of your emotions before trying to solve the problem.

It may require a herculean effort on both of your parts to disengage before the sparks begin to fly. It will only happen if you both agree to make it happen. The natural tendency is to "strike while the iron is hot." The problem is that since you became "one flesh" at the time you were married, you are only burning yourself when you burn your mate. Not a wise thing to do.

You may have been raised in the macho world that suggests you are weak or the loser if you walk away from a fight. Just the opposite is true. Anyone can give in to their rage and stay there and fight to the physical and emotional destruction of themselves and their loved ones. It takes a powerful man or woman to swallow their pride and walk away from a fight to preserve something much more valuable than their egos—their marriage.

If you agree to disengage before saying or doing anything destructive, there also needs to be an agreement that you will re-engage at some designated time in the future and resolve the issue which was too emotionally charged to handle at the time.

Fatigue is a second factor which makes resolution of problems difficult. If either or both of you are too tired to really focus on the issue, it is easy to slide off into tangential roads where mud pits provide ample ammunition for marriage-weakening battles. You will recognize immediately when you are too tired to enjoy a problem-solving session.

Have a predetermined sign to call off the discussion until you can recover from your state of fatigue. In an earlier chapter I suggested the athletic "time out" signal. You may find one that suits you better. More serious problems have been fueled with the "let's get to the bottom of this right now" attitude than one would care to admit. Perhaps standing back and taking a second look will provide you with perspective which was not available to you at the time of the initial offense. Time often provides answers to questions which, if hurried, evade the impetuous. Resolve now not to act in haste or anger or fatigue.

A third time to avoid trying to solve problems is when either or both of you are in a combative mood. It seems common to humanity to have mood swings. Some are so extreme that a person can be congenial and friendly one minute and explosive and argumentative the next. Hopefully, you are both in better control than that.

If you recognize that you are starting to look for areas in which to contend, agree to walk away until some future time. Even in the middle of what we will now describe as a problem- solving session, it is better to admit you are more interested in verbal dueling than you are in healing the rift between you. Perhaps you are more in touch with the cause of your moods than I, but there are times when I just seem to be prowling around teasing someone to disagree with me. If I could identify the source, I would eliminate that tendency from my personality. Until then, I am trying to master the art of walking away.

When a difference arises, consciously draw a distinction between the issue and the person involved. The love of your mate should never be in question even if the offense is intentional. Your love for your mate should not be conditioned on their acting in a prescribed way. Children often provide the best example of how to teach this principle. Perhaps it is leaving clothes lying around their bedroom that needs to be addressed. The issue is the dirty clothes lying around. Although the child is the perpetrator, it is more productive to focus on the issue. When discussing with the kids the picking up of the clothes, they will often revert to accusing each other for the offense. That only results in bad feelings. Even after years of experience, I find it challenging to get families to stop confessing each other's sins and refocus on the problem—the dirty clothes. I try to help the kids envision a box with the problem in it. As we combine our efforts to find a solution, each may verbally shoot at the box as often as they please and with as much gusto as they want to use. We are not interested in verbally shooting at each other. While it may be true that one or more of the kids are the basic cause of the problem, it is the problem we want "fixed," not the child.

The same holds true in marriage. There seems to be an automatic resistance and a vigorous rebuttal to personal attack. No one likes to be told they are a slob. If one of you hasn't overcome the problem of leaving clothes around the house, it is more productive to say something like: "I think we would be less embarrassed when guests come to visit if there weren't clothes lying around the house." Can you see that we are attacking the offensive issue rather than the person who leaves their clothes lying around? Since (at least in the beginning of your marriage) there are likely only two of you, it is obvious who the offender is. That does not lessen the fact that it is easier and more pleasant to tackle the issue than each other.

With a little practice, you will find it isn't too difficult to take the extra few seconds necessary to phrase your complaint against the problem and not against the person. Think back to your youth. Did your parents "nag" you for some of the things you didn't do according to their wishes? How did you feel when they "nagged" you, even when you knew that you should do better? Wouldn't you have been more responsive if they had tackled the problem without making you feel like a miserable slob?

As the problems are solved, the irritants are eliminated and harmony is restored to the home. In other words, the person gets "fixed" without being attacked when the solution to the problem is agreed upon and implemented. My wife is a master at getting me to conform to basic rules by pointing out how much better the spirit in the home would be if we all did something differently. Usually I already know she is right before she brings up the problem. If we attack the person instead of the problem, the almost universal come-back is to point out that the person making the accusation is not perfect either and follow it up with one or more examples. Hurt feelings are the most frequent result of the recriminating accusation war.

Next, separate the problem from the solution. Many don't seem to see the differences. It may require some effort on your parts to master this technique. If the problem is one that deals with your mate saying things that hurt your feelings, it may be natural to continually revert back to talking about the problem. For example, "it really hurts my feelings when my weaknesses are openly discussed with your parents." Notice we are focusing on the undesirable behavior rather than on the offender.

The next step would be to try to find an agreeable solution. "How can we break the habit?" or "What do you want me to say when my parents ask direct questions concerning you?" Those are both direct questions suggesting a desire to solve the problem. If the offended partner slides back and starts re-defining the problem, you might say, "would you like to discuss the problem some more?" If they continue, let them go on until they have defined the problem to their satisfaction. Then say, "How are we going to solve the problem?" If they haven't clearly separated in their own mind the difference between the problem and the solution, they may revert again to describing the problem. Let them go ahead and talk again about the problem. Before long they will catch on that the problem is one thing and the possible solutions are entirely different.

Children are especially susceptible to confusing the problem and the solutions. As you draw the distinction, you will find that problems are only opportunities to exercise your creative abilities to work out solutions. Those who have not practiced problem-solving often see only one solution. With a little effort you can usually find several (sometimes many!) possible solutions which add excitement and fun to the problem-solving session.

When the problem is identified—it only takes a few minutes to identify the problem, then move immediately to possible solutions. Let's take leaving the dirty dishes on the table or in the sink rather than putting them in the dishwasher and starting it. Someone is destined to become the domestic slave unless everyone participates. It is usually the wife. In one of your problem-solving sessions, the problem is identified—hopefully without tears or accusations. Now your attention can be turned to finding an agreeable solution. It isn't always the obvious solution that works best. Sure it would be nice if part of the meal included clearing the table and putting the dishes in the dishwasher.

Instead of always listing the obvious, try being a bit more creative. One of you might suggest, "I'll clear the dishes and load the dishwasher on even days of the month and you do it on the odd days." That's a possibility. Don't stop with a single possible solution. A second might be, "I'll clear the table and load the dishwasher while you put the food away and sweep the floor. We can trade jobs each week." That's a good solution. A third might be, "Why don't we work together on the dishes and the floors so we can both watch television when the work is done." That's good too. With a little effort you may be able to devise half a dozen possible solutions to the problem.

Whenever the problem-solving sessions degenerates into ripping flesh, you are contributing to the weakening of your marriage. As you master the art of separating the problem from the possible solutions, your problem-solving sessions become more fun and actually something to be anticipated.

Next is the agreeing upon a solution. It isn't much of a marriage if one partner demands that their solution be accepted all the time. As a young man I had some pretty definite ideas about how things were to be done. Unfortunately, in those early days I probably forced my solutions on others more than I ever should have. As I grew older I realized that other people have opinions and ideas too. To my utter amazement and disbelief, I learned that some of their solutions were superior to mine.

Now it is much more rewarding to talk about all possible solutions, put them on the table and consider them one at a time.

Often some of the proposed solutions are not really possible so they are discarded only after due consideration. Then the child or person making the suggestion of a possible solution knows that their ideas count and doesn't feel rejected just because the rest of the family decided not to use their suggestion. It is best when a unanimous vote can be given on a single solution. Usually with a little effort, agreement can be reached.

If you can get the entire family to "buy into" the solution, no matter what it is, it will work. When a family member senses ownership of an idea, they have a vested interest in making it work. Try forcing your idea down the throats of the family members and you'll receive lukewarm support at best. There usually isn't a single correct way of solving problems. It is a matter of selecting which would be more desirable.

Once the decision is made and agreed upon, set up a time when you will follow through to make sure the decision is implemented. Too often we decide something then just forget about it. A note on the fridge, a quick check just before going to bed, right after church meetings, just before your weekly date, almost any time is all right to make sure irritating elements in your marriage are being overcome. Don't leave accountability to one person all the time. Share the responsibility of follow-up. If your proposed solution is mutually agreed upon, then you can each remind the other of your commitment. Then, two heads really are better at remembering than one.

This topic seems so very simple. It is! However, wars have been and continue to be fought over people's unwillingness to attack the problems rather than each other. Living in a daily war zone seems to me to be less than an ideal marital setting. That problems will arise seems to be a given. However, when both of you decide to focus on and eliminate the problem rather than each other, love and solidarity replace hatred and dissolution of your marriage. The results are more than worth the effort necessary.

7

BEING TRUE TO EACH OTHER

— ❤ —

We live in a world where activity is equated with progress. Although progress often requires activity, all activity is definitely not progress. One needs only to review the skyrocketing occurrences of divorce during the last half century to see that couples are far less likely to enjoy a lifetime together now than they were when our grandparents were first married. Although there is no one answer that neatly identifies a simple cause, there are alarming trends which notably parallel the escalating rise in divorce. One such trend is unfaithfulness in marriage.

Movies glamorize extra-marital affairs. Premarital sexual experience seems to be accepted as one of the facts of life. Not so many years ago these basic premises were not viewed as a given or accepted generally by society. Even though there seems to be a large segment of the population who glory in publicly displaying their unfaithfulness, the media is less likely to give equal time to the millions who are being true to the promises they made at the marital altar.

If you are willing to accept either premarital sex or extra-marital sex as normal or unavoidable, perhaps you have arrived at the point where continuing to read this book would be a waste of time. Since we are discussing a "divorce-less marriage," we are not looking at the norm or average relationship. We are focusing on the extra-ordinary, the rare, the atypical—but we are also looking at the achievable, the desirable, the ideal. Perhaps we can investigate more closely some underlying principles which strongly vote in favor of total abstinence before marriage and absolute fidelity in marriage.

In order to endure, a relationship must be built upon a foundation of mutual trust. That trust has two prongs: (1) trust in each other; and (2) trust in one's self. As you begin the courtship process, you are taking two very different individuals and developing a foundation of common beliefs and values. As you are well aware, not every relationship ends in marriage. Generally, before very many dates, a couple can determine whether sufficient common interests, goals, and values exist to warrant continuing the relationship. Most dating relationships end after a couple of encounters. This does not suggest the "goodness" or "badness" of a person. It only recognizes the different chemistries people have.

The relationships which endure are those where both partners can begin to see sufficient common ground upon which to build a stable relationship. When couples have strictly a hormonal relationship (i.e. a strong sexual attraction for each other), they may either become sexually involved or actually move towards marriage. Unfortunately, the glue which makes for enduring relationships must have a broader application than just sex. After the newness of the honeymoon has worn off, it is natural (and desirable) to begin to rely more on other aspects of your relationship other than just your physical attraction for each other. If you don't have anything but your sexual attraction, your marriage is in trouble from the very first. Not to be misunderstood, sexual attractions need to be powerful and more or less constant, but standing alone, they do not make for an enduring relationship.

No doubt there are some very strong sexual feelings between the two of you or chances are you would have terminated the relationship long before. When you restrain yourself from taking sexual liberties with each other, it develops a sense of trust between you.

In marriage you may have promised to love, cherish, honor, and obey one another until death separated you. If you have established a trust with yourself and with your mate, being true to each other is merely a continuation of that which you started before marriage. If you were sexually involved before marriage, it is not impossible to develop that trust after the wedding, but it is more difficult. It requires that you decide once and for all that your eyes will not wander to another person. It requires that no one or no thing will come between you.

There is no question that temptations will come. When you are separated for business trips or training sessions, it is difficult to refrain from looking at other men or woman who are dressed to the "T" and seem to be totally void of the responsibilities associated with home and family. When you are required to work closely with someone of the opposite sex on a daily basis, it is too easy to start to share intimate information with them. Remember, the sharing of intimacies before marriage was also the way you started developing your trust relationship which resulted in marriage.

Although stories of unfaithfulness by husbands and wives in the work place abound, it is also true that millions of married men and women work closely with each other without becoming sexually involved. Part of the trust factor is being able to trust yourself when you are away from your mate. In part, that trust was developed by your physically restraining yourself before marriage.

How do you work closely with people of the opposite sex at the office or in the work place and not become involved? Be true to your commitment to each other. Refuse to entertain a first thought about becoming involved. I teach at a major university where I interface on a daily basis with the most beautiful girls in the world. When I never allow myself to consider becoming involved with them, it isn't difficult to be true to my wife and family. I keep a picture of my wife and children prominently displayed in my office. When young women come in to counsel, I have to look right past my wife's picture to see them. It isn't difficult to stay focused on the love of my life when her picture is always in front of me.

It is when men or women experience difficulties at home that the facade of glamour, no responsibility, and ease at the office become enticing. When problems are solved at home and efforts are made to make home a bit more like heaven, then the allurements at the office hold few, if any, enticements. When attention and affection are shared at home on a regular basis and the flame of love is constantly fanned, there is little or no enticement to find romantic fulfillment outside the home. It seems ironical that as young people we would give such rapt attention to feeding the fire while out camping. No one questioned the advisability of keeping the fire fueled while on a winter camp. Then viewed as a campfire, why would we think it less important to keep fueling the fires of romance? Left to itself, the campfire would soon die out and only smoking embers would remain. The same holds true in marriage. Left without constant attention, the flaming fire of romance soon becomes smoking, smoldering, eye-irritating embers.

The failure to attend to a camp fire certainly does not infer that the fire was defective. The fact that many couples allow the fire of romance to become smoldering, eye-irritating embers does not mean that the marriage was bad or should never have been engaged in initially. The constant thinking about, working to improve, being faithful in marriage, all keep the flames of romance burning brightly.

One problem that affects relationships in the home is a lack of publicized role models. Too much of what Hollywood produces gives the false impression of what love and marriage really is. If you indulge yourselves to an excess in that fantasy world, it will begin to breed discontentment in your own relationship. Artificial expectations are not realistic. Merely following the headlines on the tabloids clearly demonstrates that many of those who act the parts in the great romance movies are no more successful in having a heavenly marriage than anyone else. Be careful when looking for role models in marriage. If a false standard is used to measure your marriage relationship, disappointment and discontentment will surely follow.

If you find your mind and eyes wandering from your mate, early recognition is the most essential factor. Admit to yourself that you are starting to have romantic inclination towards someone. It would be better for you to disassociate with them immediately if you are unable to control your feelings. If it is not possible to separate your working environments, then it requires double effort and constant vigilance to control the situation. The fact that many millions of people do control their feelings while working closely with members of the opposite sex is sufficient testimonial that it can be done. You might consider focusing on something other than your relationship. Don't dwell on either thinking about the person or thinking about not thinking about the person. In either case you are constantly thinking about the person. Instead, when you realize your mind is thinking about them, let that act as a catalyst to get you to refocus on thinking about your mate and children. If that doesn't work, think about your favorite hobby, sport, or interest. Thankfully, our minds are so designed that we are not able to really focus on more than one thing at a time. By you taking a pro-active approach to controlling your thoughts, you will happily discover that you, not the environment, determines what you think and how you act.

One of the great cop-outs of our day is to believe that the environment controls the organism. While your environment does have an impact on you, it does not have an uncontrollable influence on your behavior. Don't look at yourself as a victim because you are compelled to work in close proximity with someone of the opposite sex who has some appeal to you.

If nothing else works, talk to your supervisor and ask for a change of assignments. Having lived over five decades, I have concluded that I would rather start all over with a new job rather than keep my tenured position where I presently work and ruin my marriage. Seldom will it be necessary to change jobs to avoid contact with a distracting person. If it is, what is the level of commitment to your marriage partner and family?

You may have grown up with the idea that with the passage of time, you will become bored with each other sexually. While many couples seem to suffer from that condition, it is not a given. Many couples look back at those early sexual experiences and realize that what they though was love could be more accurately described as lust. With the passage of years, the breadth and scope of affections often increases in all areas. Sex at fifty is often much more mutually fulfilling than honeymoon sex. For the young that may be a difficult concept to imagine. For those who have endured the trials of life together and have an almost perfect trust in each other, they will immediately see the truth of the statement.

Broken trusts in marriage are difficult (but not impossible!) to reestablish. If mistakes are made, it will require the greatest effort of your life to forgive, forget, and move on. Too many marriages do not have the stability to weather such a devastating storm. If unfaithfulness has occurred, you should reestablish the ground rules and start from the bottom up in rebuilding those bridges of trust and love. I have seen instances where couples have weathered the unfaithfulness storm and had a happy life. Unfortunately, more often I have seen marriages that did not survive the storm. Resolve now to avoid the approaches to infidelity and you will never have to discover first-hand whether your marriage can survive or not.

8

SOLVING PROBLEMS WITHOUT ARGUING

— ♥ —

As children, many of us grew up believing that "might makes right!" Whoever could bully or intimidate the other or shout the loudest or use the most shocking language won the argument. Unfortunately, many adults never grew out of that childish stage. Even more unfortunate for us all, many of those adults have become leaders of nations who still employ the same tactics to achieve their selfish desires. Our objective in this chapter is not to solve the problems of the world but to help you avoid the marriage-threatening results of arguing with each other.

As with all other principles discussed in this book, you must start with a mutually agreed-upon foundation. If you both agree that you will not argue, you have made the first giant step towards living in peace and harmony. This is another one of those "whether you think you can or you can't, you are right" situations. If, as a couple, you do not believe it is possible to live together for a lifetime without arguing, you are correct. Not because it is impossible, but because you will not expend the energy and self-restraint necessary to make something happen that you think is impossible. If, on the other hand, you envision a marriage free of bitter arguments, and, if you are willing to work together to make it happen, it is very likely that you will enjoy a battle-free marriage.

Because we made the commitment nearly thirty years ago and have stuck to it, I choose to use our marriage as an example. We are not, however, the only ones who have made it work. I have challenged students for almost thirty years to try establishing an argument-free marriage. Not a few have reported back after five, ten, twenty years and said it is working fine for them. How is it done?

I am not interested in giving some "pie-in-the-sky" formula that is simply not achievable. Being a died-in-the-wool pragmatist, if it is broke you fix it and if it ain't broke you leave it alone. Without being obvious, I have just given the philosophy for success in battle-free marriage. In order to know whether something is broke, you must have an understanding of how it should be when it "ain't broke."

To be more specific, couples do not fight over issues they agree upon. Think about it. Those areas of conflict arise when we have differing opinions about something upon which we have not come to a prior agreement. Then the obvious solution is that we create or establish agreement in as many areas as we possibly can before marriage or early in marriage so the occasions to disagree are fewer.

How do you identify those areas of possible conflict? Separately and together sit down and review your pasts. Where have your major conflicts with family and friends started? It may have been that you had some serious arguments with your friends over rules of a game. If there had been total agreement about the rules and their interpretation, there wouldn't have been a battlefield for the ensuing argument. Perhaps major battles occurred within the family over chores and the division of labor. Had a family council been convened and dad or mom clearly spelled out the chores, occasions for accusations of unfairness might have been significantly decreased or eliminated altogether.

The more accurately you identify those areas of potential conflict, the easier it is to discuss plans for dealing with them long before they happen. When the television is turned off or the video goes unwatched, the opportunities to talk about potentially difficult situations greatly increase. As you interface day by day, observation of others and situations which arise in your own lives often remind you of areas you want to address. By being aware and keeping a constant vigilance during your courtship, many problematic areas can be successfully addressed before they ever arise.

You may be thinking, "Not everything can be decided beforehand." While I am the first to admit the truth of that statement, I also realize that most couples have not taken the time to identify and resolve possible areas of conflict nearly to the degree they could if they were serious about avoiding confrontations. Before closing the door on this subject, give it a try and see if your attention to details does not significantly reduce the tension between you. As I mentioned before, I am after workable solutions, so let's move on.

When there are personal differences in preferences, tastes, or wants, it isn't always a matter of coming to a pre-agreement to avoid conflict. At the grocery store I may want chocolate ice cream and my wife may favor vanilla. Since the freezer (our waist lines and our budget too!) will only accommodate one container of ice cream, we must choose. You are probably way ahead of me. Why not just buy Neapolitan ice cream and we can both fulfill our wants without either having to sacrifice? Many of the apparent conflicts we experience are not conflicts at all. They merely require some mental gymnastics to figure out how to satisfy both wants.

A while back we took our family to Europe for a family vacation. Getting ten strong-willed people to agree on anything required a lot of diplomacy. One of the issues was "where do you want to eat?" The older children saw the opportunity to eat native food at some fine restaurants. The younger children wanted to seek out the nearest McDonald's. There was no way I intended to travel halfway around the world to eat at McDonald's. But the younger children felt strongly about their right to have a voice in the matter. The solution was so simple. We either took them to McDonald's and left them to eat, or let them eat first and then they played in a park close to the restaurant where we chose to eat. Surprisingly, we had no conflicts in three weeks because we found that almost always we could accommodate everyone's wants.

You may ask, "What if you can't always do what everyone wants to do?" That's a valid question. As young married, strong-willed people, we devised a two-prong approach to the potential problem. First we prioritized our wants. I did not always get to do what I wanted to do. If my wife had something higher on her priority list than mine, she got her way. If you are genuinely trying to put your mate first, this becomes a pleasant game. As kids come along, the difficulty of prioritizing becomes more challenging. Perhaps that is why children start to leave home for school, work, or marriage about the time it becomes too taxing to weigh everyone's priorities.

It really doesn't make much difference to me where we go out to eat on our weekly date. Food is something I eat in order to live. However, my wife has very fine tastes and very definite preferences. Therefore, it is easy for me to subject my preferences to hers. I win no matter where we go because we like the same kinds of food—with one major exception (pizza!). When I willingly allow her to choose where to eat, she reciprocates by allowing me to choose what activity we engage in. She is a good sport so we can go to a football game in the snow or bowling or hiking, or whatever, even though she would prefer to go to a movie or a play. Don't get the idea that I always get my way in what we do.

The second prong of the approach eliminates the chances of one person always getting his or her way because of how strongly they feel about a certain activity. We use a rotating system of selecting whose priorities take precedence. If I really want to go to a football game and my wife really wants to go to a play, it is not possible to do both because they occur at the same time. Then we may flip a coin or "choose a number between one and a hundred," or use some other way of deciding whose preference we do. Then the next time an unresolvable conflict arises, we automatically go with the other partner. As we learn to give and take, it becomes less frequent when we have strong disagreeing preferences.

Using the rotating system of choosing definitely means that you won't always get your way in marriage. At first glance everyone will readily agree that they don't expect to get their way all the time. However, as is evident from so many marriages at risk, one or both partners may lose their spirit of compromise and sacrifice after the honeymoon is over.

Let's return to the basic premise for a few minutes. The more you understand each other before marriage or in those very early days following the wedding, the fewer areas of potential conflict exist. I would seriously doubt that it is possible to anticipate every situation where conflict might arise. So "how" you handle those conflicts becomes as important as whether you have them or not.

Many years ago as a young college student, I was enrolled in the ROTC (Reserve Officer's Training Corps). As part of our training we spent six weeks at an infantry basic training camp at Fort Benning, Georgia. During our training we were taken to a remote area where the army had constructed a complex of obstacle training courses. The individual obstacles were designed so that it required the cooperation of the entire group to accomplish the task in the designated amount of time. If we did not work together or if we did not use our time and resources wisely, the buzzer ending the session would sound before we had completed the obstacle and we received no points for our efforts.

The same is true in marriage. There are so many obstacles in our path that require singular cooperation that we can't complete the task unless we work together. Not allowing problems to divide you or cause you to be adversarial is a key issue. Every marriage is given exactly the same amount of a singular commodity—time. The rich don't have any more of it than the poor. The illiterate have the same amount as the educated. The diligent don't have any more than the overly casual. How to allocate your time is the more important consideration.

Some marriages start with more physical resources than others. You may think that they have a definite advantage. Reading the newspaper and watching television reports about the problems of the rich leads me to believe that it isn't how much money a person has that makes the difference but how he or she uses it. Mutual agreement on how to use both time and resources are huge contributing factors to the success of your scoring the maximum points on each obstacle course.

Although the honeymoon is a wonderful time to sit back and really enjoy each other, if it were to continue indefinitely both parties would soon tire and start looking for something else to do. Life seems to be designed to provide multiple opportunities for problem-solving. In fact without naturally occurring challenges, we often manufacture them. For me, the ultimate punishment would be to lock me in a prison cell with absolutely nothing to do. From the accounts of those who have suffered that fate, it is evident that they immediately start devising methods of escape—overcoming a seemingly unsurmountable obstacle.

In chapter 13 we will give attention to how to confront the obstacles of life without becoming disagreeable. For this chapter, let us conclude by stating that your attitude towards problems is essential in successfully meeting those challenges. If you view troubles and problems as a sign of failure, your marriage will be on the rocks before you know it. If, on the other hand, you see obstacles and problems as challenges which are exciting and growth producing, you will learn to thrive on them. No, you do not need to go looking for problems—they seem to find you without any effort on your part. But to shy away from them when they are inescapable would not be a proper response.

Since problems are part of what life is made up of, learn to enjoy the experience. What a thrill not to have to face the problems alone. Now you have someone of your own choosing, who (hopefully) is your equal, with when to surmount every problem. Enjoy the challenge.

9

Being "Other" Oriented

— ♥ —

A great philosopher once said: "Divorce is a totally selfish act where two people consider no one other than themselves individually." I have thought a lot about that statement. Especially where children are concerned, I can see where he is coming from. In three decades of working with adolescents and young adults, it is abundantly evident that divorce destroys not only their parents' marriage but their entire world. As I have counseled with men and women who have suffered the trauma of divorce, his statement is again reinforced. When I have occasion to listen to the extended families of those who have divorced, I again find his words verified. Divorce is a selfish act. Having said that, how can the dread disease be prevented?

If we accept the premise that divorce is caused in part by being self-centered, it seems obvious that to focus our attention outward would contribute to the demise of divorce. When a person focuses on meeting the needs of other people, offenses (intended or innocent) are not taken so seriously. When your major concern is in meeting the needs of others, you become less aware of whether all of your needs are being met.

A number of years ago a young divorced mother of three sat in my office wringing her hands and sobbing. She was at her wits' end. She claimed that she didn't have the energy, either mental or physical, to exist for another day. I felt a sincere empathy for her. I have felt that way many times when the burdens of life seemed to be piled high on my shoulders. I almost surprised myself by saying: "Why don't you forget the obvious fact that your needs are not being met? Go home and play with your children. Make a game of cleaning up the house. Take them shopping with you and make them miniature shoppers. Send them on missions to find the items on your shopping list. Make sandwiches and eat supper in the park. Let them play on the playground. Watch them play and think how much each of them means to you and how absolutely vital you are in their lives. Take them home and put them to bed. Read them a story if they want you to. Don't think another thought about yourself and your needs. See how you feel in the morning."

She looked at me with the same shocked expression of unbelief that I was feeling on the inside. I think she was so taken back that she didn't have anything to say. I asked her to call and report the next day. To my utter amazement, she called the next day and was a totally new woman. The zest was back in her voice and the bounce in her step. She said she felt like she had experienced a total rejuvenation. Somehow the vital energy (emotional and physical) that she so desperately needed was replenished as she forgot herself and focused on those who depended on her. Certainly her problems were not completely solved. But both she and I learned a new technique. Since that day, I have used that counsel often and almost always with positive results.

Following that initial episode, I started to gather personal data about the "serve to be renewed" phenomenon. I noticed in my own life that when I had a speaking engagement or some other obligation that I couldn't get out of, no matter how badly I felt, if I went ahead with the obligation, invariably I felt physically and mentally stronger when it was over. I once watched an elderly church leader stand to give a presentation after apologizing for feeling ill. I thought we would have to pick him up after he passed out. By the time he was fifteen minutes into his presentation, his voice was strong and he seemed to be suffering no ill effects from his sickness.

There seems to be something rejuvenating about revitalizing others even when our gas gage is on empty. Try it and see if it works for you.

As you turn your focus towards your mate a wonderful thing starts to happen. You become more interested in meeting his or her needs than you are in having your needs met. When you totally lose yourself in meeting their needs, another miracle often occurs. They, in turn, reciprocate by trying to more fully meet your needs. The more they focus on meeting your needs, the more reinforcement that comes from the above principle and the stronger your relationship grows.

Some "experts" maintain that marriage should be a 50-50 proposition, with an equal sharing of everything from housework to earning income to caring for children. I can't think of any arrangement that would be more subject to disaster. Let me explain. If you enter into a 50-50 agreement (which totals 100%) and either of you falls just one percent short, there is a gap in your marriage. Into that gap the unseen adversary of all marriages drives the first wedge. Over time, because we are human, we may fall short again and again. Each time a wedge is driven between us. Before long we are sufficiently separated by the accumulation of these wedges that our marriage is unstable and subject to dissolution.

It seems more practical to have a 100-100 marriage. When I give 100% to my wife and she gives 100% to me, then even if we were to both fail by 10% we would still have an 80% coverage! Does this seem too idealistic? It has worked for us and continues to work for hundreds of couples I have counseled with over the years.

You might ask, "What happens if one partner gives 100% and the other doesn't give at all?" I readily admit that over time that would seriously weaken a marriage. But, as mentioned before, if you establish this giving relationship before the wedding or shortly thereafter, the likelihood of one partner being a 100% taker while their spouse is a 100% giver is very remote.

More often the opposite of selfishness happens—selflessness. A selfish person would immediately criticize this plan as idealistic and not realistic. That is because they are always concerned about having their own needs met. A person who has experienced the joy of self-less service is less inclined to criticize the suggestion.

Three decades ago my wife and I started trying to "one upmanship" each other. In retrospect, I am sure she started the game. She did something nice for me for no reason other than to express her love. Not to be outdone, I tried to do something a little nicer than she had done. Not to be bested, she did something even nicer for me. Refusing to come in second, I mustered all of my creativity and came up with something extra good for her. This has been going on for thirty years. Every once in a while I will totally take her by surprise. She was expecting our third child and was being run ragged by the other two children. I secretly bought her a plane ticket, got her released for a few days from the responsibilities of being a mom (I signed the release papers!), got the documents necessary to cover babysitting (from her mother and mine), arranged for a substitute for her Church calling, gave her an envelope with spending money, and sent her off for a few days to visit her sister in Arizona. She was so surprised and overcome, I was afraid she was going to deliver early! The look of surprise, satisfaction, joy, relief, and thanksgiving on her face was worth the weeks of secretive planning I had done. I won big!

A selfish person might ask: "If you did all that for her, how can you say you won big? She got all the benefit!" Anyone who has served realizes the truth of the old adage: "It is more blessed to give than to receive." After her return home, she immediately went to work doing a hundred nice things for me. From then on it has been nearly impossible to keep up with her thoughtfulness. My thoughtful gesture lasted for only a few days. Her selfless service has played itself out for years. I really was the short-term and long-term winner.

Growing up I could never figure out why it was more fun to mow my friends' lawns than my own. Now I have discovered that we can all have fun if we just agree to mow each other's lawns. In marriage it is the same. Doing boring, mundane jobs that you must do has few or no elements of fun. Doing those same mundane chores for someone you love is fun and exciting. How could you possibly enjoy focusing inward when the real joys of life come from focusing outward?

You can tell when you are approaching the level of "Master Server" when you find yourself constantly wondering what you can do next to please your mate. It is equally as easy to determine when you are losing ground as you wonder why people aren't meeting your needs more effectively.

When a person expects someone to do something for them, and the other person fails to perform, there are always feelings of frustration and sometimes betrayal. When expectations for service are not there and yet a service is performed, profound feelings of gratitude often result. Therefore, it seems more productive to give more and expect less, thus reducing the frustration levels and increasing the gratitude level. Although that may sound somewhat philosophical, in reality it is simple and beautiful. Why? Because in life there are many times when we come to expect people to perform at a level they have committed to and they do not. If we become irritated at their failure to perform, we spend a good part of our life upset. I am not suggesting that we lose faith in people or fail to expect them to perform according to commitment, but I am saying that you can buffer yourself against feelings of anger and frustration if you seize the opportunity to serve beyond the level of normal expectation. You, then, become the source of generating feelings of gratitude and appreciation. In marriage those feelings of gratitude and appreciation are like super glue which cement husband to wife and parents to children. As weakening and destructive as the feelings of anger and frustration are, the opposite is true of love and thankfulness.

When a person becomes obsessed with their own selfish wants and desires, they emit invisible signals which repel others. My experience has been that no one is particularly fond of being around an egocentric person. One who constantly demands the spotlight or center stage, is seldom the first one on the invitation list for a party. In marriage the egotist rapidly wears on the feelings and patience of his or her partner.

Contrary to what one may believe, the more you do for others, the more you give away, the more of you there is to give. Capitalistic economics may suggest the opposite. They may consider that there is a limited amount of you—time, talent, resource, etc. Therefore the more you expend, the less of you there is. Somehow they fail to understand the regenerating and renewing effect that selfless service has on the giver. Perhaps the world will never understand that one vital lesson which is so essential to happy marriages. That is, there is more room in the spotlight than one person can possibly fill. The more people you succeed in drawing into the spotlight, the larger the spot becomes. There is room at center stage for an infinite number of people.

So when the world teaches you that there is only room at the top for one, they demonstrate their failure to see things as they really are. The better my wife looks, the better she makes me look. The more praise and notoriety she receives, the more honor comes to me. The more noble I can help her become, the more she ennobles me. I would be a fool of the first order if I did anything other than focus my improving efforts on her.

If it is total success that you desire in marriage, focus on your partner one hundred percent. Watch the richness of your life surpass anything you have ever seen in your marriage or any other person's marriage (unless of course they have used the same philosophy). True happiness does not come in having your needs met—it comes from helping meet the needs of others. Try it.

10

GIVING ATTENTION TO THE LITTLE THINGS

— ❤ —

At first glance you may assume from the chapter title that we will be talking about birthdays, holidays, and anniversaries. Obviously you should give them due consideration. If they are ignored, it could result in marital stress. However, I have chosen to focus on several different areas. Some may be as obvious as those mentioned, others may not be so readily identifiable.

I have noticed a basic difference between meetings where the person in charge of the physical arrangements is a man and those where the person in charge is a woman. Most men will have arranged for the very basics: chairs, a table, glasses of water, a lectern, and lighting. When a woman is in charge, all the basics will also be covered but there will likely be a tablecloth on the table with a centerpiece artfully done. Water glasses will be placed on a coaster or napkin and perhaps will have a slice of lemon in them. The lectern will have a banner announcing the organization hosting the meeting. There may be soft music playing in the background. Often there is attention given to the natural lighting from the windows contrasted with the artificial lighting from within the room.

What is the difference? The attention to details. However, the net results are often profound. Contracts are won, relationships cemented, and business prosperity increases when every detail is carefully attended to. Marriages are not too different from business deals. You can get by with just the basics: living together, sleeping together, eating together, working, and socializing. Many marriages are about that sterile. If you want a full, rich marriage, try giving more attention to the little details.

Working can be and often is a drudgery. It has to be done because money doesn't usually grow on trees. Sack lunches can become as boring as work with little or no effort. What a thrill to open the lunch pail and find a "love note." Nothing elaborate, just a little "I was thinking of you and am so glad we are married!" One note like that can change the entire day. It cost little or nothing but the dividends are incalculable. One telephone call home from work "just to say 'Hi' because I was thinking of you" can take the mundane drudgery out of housework. It only takes a minute and usually doesn't cost a cent, but it not only revolutionizes your mate's day but may actually enhance your enjoyment of your otherwise boring work.

Whenever I go out of town on a speaking engagement, I can count on notes being in my shaving kit, in my socks, in my underwear, in my suit pockets, even in the notes for my talk. One time I was sitting on the stand waiting for the meeting to begin and happened to open my talk notes for a quick review. There prominently displayed was a post-it which read: "You'll do great! Wish I was in the audience to enjoy your talk! Love you." I became a little embarrassed as I noticed the person in charge of the meeting reading my note. I quickly pocketed the note and said nothing. When the presiding officer introduced me, he made reference to the note and then made a parenthetical comment: "I wish my wife gave me reinforcement like that." Then turning to me he said: "I hope you never take for granted how fortunate you are to have a wife like that!"

What I sometimes take for granted are some of the very things that make our marriage run smoothly. I resolved then never to overlook the little things. With some constant vigilance, you can become much more aware of how many things your mate does for you. Merely drawing your attention to the issue should make you more attentive.

Although it would be exposing yourself to possible disappointment to expect your mate or anyone else to recognize everything you do, it is rewarding and reinforcing to have your special someone compliment you on work you have done. If the furniture is moved around, or a messy closet cleaned out, or the flower bed weeded and planted, or a thousand other like "little things," it costs nothing to keep your eyes open and say something nice. "Boy, you must have worked all day long on that closet! It was really a disaster area. You've worked wonders!" Verbal salve like that may not eliminate the aching back or the bruised muscles, but it sure warms the soul and makes the sacrifices worthwhile.

Although it may sound like I am talking directly to the husband (and I probably am!), compliments going in the other direction are equally as appreciated. The washing of the car and vacuuming it out on the way home from work is easy to overlook. Of course he ought to do it without expecting to be praised. But the rewards resulting from a word of appreciation will reinforce his efforts to make the car more pleasant for the entire family. "Gee, the car looks nice. You can't imagine how much I appreciate you vacuuming up the chips and Cheerio's the kids dropped the other day. It was beginning to smell like a feed yard!" Didn't cost a cent to say, but the solidifying dollars that it earned made for a good investment in your marriage account.

Often we become so engrossed in our own lives and problems, that we fail to notice the haircut, the new dress, the special supper, the favorite video rented, the five pounds that have been dropped, the compliment received, the prompt payment of bills, or any of a thousand other little things. Sure, we expect those things to happen and they probably will whether we say anything or not, but the feelings between you and your mate will be deepened and enriched if you do remember to notice.

In spite of the fact that you may have been aware and actually given attention to many of the above-listed items, there are still other "little things" which contribute to a smooth running marriage. Let's look at the little things that make the difference between the really good marriage and those which are just surviving.

My wife is very socially adept. I am learning by sad experience that it would be better if I would give more attention to being more aware in trying to be socially correct. Because my circle of acquaintances includes some very influential people, I could be much more concerned if my wife was the type of person who engaged her mouth before her mind. Saying the wrong thing at the wrong time at some of those high level meetings could irreparably damage my career. Occasionally I will say (in total honesty), "I am so proud to have you with me. You always make me look so good to my associates!" I thought I was just stating the obvious until she sat quietly for a few miles after I had made the comment and then said: "Do you have any idea how good your compliment made me feel?" The honest answer was "no!" Then it dawned on me that I receive compliments all the time because of my speeches and presentations. It is not as common for her to be in the limelight. What was a statement of fact for me was a supreme compliment for her. It didn't cost a cent but it sure made a difference in our marriage. Don't neglect to praise what seems obvious to you.

Late one evening, my wife and I had been working through some difficult decisions. Both of us were dog tired and ready for bed. As we leaned on each other for support, she said, "I'm really glad I married you. I don't know how I could have figured all this out on my own." Again, to her it was probably a statement of fact. For me, it was a compliment that made the struggles and headaches justifiable.

Perhaps the principle here is: "Don't assume that what is obvious to you is automatically obvious to your mate." If you want him or her to know something you appreciate about them, say it. I don't know whether it was in jest or not, but a friend confided to me that her husband had made the following comment after she inquired whether he really loved her: "I told you I loved you when we got married. If I ever change my mind, I'll let you know!" I can only hope he was kidding, but whether he was or wasn't, in one thoughtless comment he destroyed her self-esteem and seriously weakened their marriage. Perhaps his statement represented his true feelings. But how about her feelings and needs? If she is (as she confided to me that she is) the kind of person who needs constant reinforcement, he is about as far from meeting her needs as a married couple can be. Unless he corrects his egocentric ways, his marriage will be mediocre at best and more likely in danger of dissolution.

Perhaps you are not as demonstrative in matters of affection as your mate. If you are really sincere about making your marriage work, you will consider his or her needs before your own style of doing things. Just a little word of love and encouragement may not do a thing for you, but it may be all that is necessary for your mate to keep going.

There are (and likely always will be) the "down side" of our daily lives. If we become to engrossed in keeping our own ship afloat, it is easy to miss the downtrodden look, the tear-stained cheek, the hunched shoulders, or the silent, forlorn glance. A very little "How are things going?" can open the door to allow some frustrations to be talked through. It may require a little of your time and attention, but what a relief to the overwhelmed.

Often it is not necessary to say anything. Just listen. In so many instances I long ago lost count, people come to my office and "unload." At the end of their catharsis, they often thank me for all my help and leave totally renewed. I sit musing in my office. I haven't done anything, solved any of their problems, or given any direction. The problems they faced when they came in to see me are still there. Nothing has changed—only that in talking the problems through they have been able to mentally organize them in such a way that they didn't seem so unconquerable. A few minutes of acting as a sounding board costs so very little but means so much.

Occasionally listening is not enough. Listening carefully enough to understand where they are coming from and then offering your very best suggestions may not directly answer their problems but it may trigger a thought that will enable them to solve their own problems. You may be saying, "I am not a professional counselor." While that is probably true, it is also true that you have gained experience every day of your life that others may not have had yet. What seems so obvious to you may be a total mystery to your mate. For example, on many occasions my wife will say something like, "I marvel at you. Where do you get all your wisdom? You always seem to know exactly what to say to help people solve their problems." While I readily admit that she exaggerates, I also realize that I have had a lot of experience which is similar to the situations others are struggling through. Search your memory for experiences which are parallel to their problems and identify principles that you have employed that worked for you to give good solid counsel. With a little practice, you will discover that there are few, if any, new problems being faced by mankind that haven't been around for centuries. True, they didn't have computers, videos, etc. centuries ago, but the basic principles behind the problems have changed but very little.

One final category of "little things" should be touched upon before concluding this chapter. The little things which surrounded us every day. The beauty of a sunset, the marvel of little birds in the spring time, the rushing of a mighty river, the waves on the seashore, all lend themselves to a shared expression of wonder. When all we see is the ugly and dark around us, it is easy to lose perspective. When we share the beauties with each other, it not only draws our mutual attention to something beautiful but it lets each of us know that the other is looking for the good in the world around us.

Again, I must admit that my wife is better at this than I am. She sees the beauty in the clouds, the trees, the fuzzy caterpillars, the wind whipping up dust in the field, the melting of ice, etc. *ad infinitum*. She has blessed my life greatly. Rather than just be on the receiving end all the time of her "did you notice . . . ," I have started to look more closely so I can share with her once in a while some of the wonders I spotted first. Our family has started celebrating summer and winter solstice and spring and fall equinox. We make fools of ourselves because my wife seldom remembers when they are. We bake cakes, get balloons, etc. and then sit back and revel at her incredulous reaction as we tell her what the big occasion is. She ruined it last fall—she remembered and called and reminded me of "what day it was." What a source of wonderment and joy, not to overlook the "little things" that surround us every day.

So shared feelings, observed marvels, mutual thoughts, collective discoveries, and common experiences all provide a very fertile seed bed for building a castle of "little things" that enrich lives and marriages no matter when they occur. You can live together and never really know each other. You can collectively experience the little things of life and discover that it isn't the big, news making events that mold your lives but those often encountered, savored "little things" that bring richness and joy to your lives.

Having just completed watching another collegiate football season at this writing, I am wondering how many people fail to realize that it isn't the nationally televised catching of the winning touchdown at the final buzzer that makes the man. Seldom is the real person revealed in such giant but rare moments. What is that person (pass receiver) like during the moments when the media does not have a camera stuck in his face? How considerate is he as a husband and father?

One begins to wonder if the professional athletes consider success a function of how much money they make. Unless their behavior is entirely different in day-to-day life than it is when they are before the television cameras, they are the most impoverished of all people in spite of their huge salaries. The real beauty of character is only discovered in the quiet serenity of marital and family trust.

How kind and considerate and attentive are you when no one is watching? Therein lies the greatness of the individual. Living outside yourself in doing for others, in being aware of their needs and trying to meet them, in lending a sympathetic ear when things are not going well, and in complimenting others for their successes are all indicators that you are more to be applauded for greatness than the egocentric slob who makes millions of dollars and has developed none of the characteristics which make for a refined human being. Build your marriage on the small little stones of mutual improvement and see how much more firm your foundation is than those who rely on the touchdown pass for recognition and approval.

11

PRIVACY ABOUT PRIVATE MATTERS

— ♥ —

Sometimes in our enthusiasm to share with others our joy and happiness, we cross over the line of propriety. Some things are meant to be shared and others are not. Only the two of you can determine which items fall into each category. We have already touched on the necessity of keeping intimate sexual matters private. Although the world seems to be obsessed with prying open closed bedroom doors, it only cheapens your relationship to put on public display those very private matters.

There is a term on many college and high school campuses with which the older generation may not be familiar. It is called "PDA's"— public displays of affection. When, as a couple, you ignore the impact you have on other people, it labels you as insensitive. There are many things you may have the "legal" right to do, which would be better undone. For example, a good-bye kiss as the wife drops the husband off at work or vice versa is usually not condemned by anyone. The deep, extended passionate kiss often experienced as a prelude to physical intimacy, however, may be labeled as inappropriate.

Unbridled passion in public suggests lack of self-restraint and also a dearth of proper teaching by your parents. I don't know if anyone has written a book about "PDA's," but they are so frequently violated that a return to the more conservative might be something the entire world would welcome. If you are the kind that sees nothing wrong with PDA's, perhaps you might watch for those expressions of intimacy which make you uncomfortable and then extend that same feeling to others who may prefer that private matters be kept private. We are generally talking about "degree" rather than the presence or absence of PDA's. Being sensitive to the thresholds of propriety of others and being willing to sacrifice your personal liberties so as not to offend them labels you as a socially sensitive person.

Assuming that you have tuned into what I am suggesting, let me broaden the field. Sometimes experiences are shared between husband and wife which are meaningful and sacred to them but may mean little or nothing to the general population. We have become a world of people who seem to revel in making light of sacred things. For example, note how many jokes take very lightly using in vain the name of God or Christ. Whether you are religiously oriented or not, to disregard that which others hold sacred does not speak well for your social breeding.

You may be thinking, "If I modify my entire behavior according to the needs of those around me, won't I be sacrificing my own personality and having my own rights trampled on?" The question is legitimate but the answer is that in reality very few things really offend most people. There are those who will be offended at your hairstyle, jewelry, clothing, etc. and even those who don't care for the way you breathe. Those people are few and far between and are destined to spend their entire lives offended because of their harsh, intolerable attitude. In general, people are fairly liberal in what they allow others to do without being offended.

Equally as appalling to those who prefer to hold the intimate relations of husband and wife as very private are the endless jokes about sex. If loose sexual talk were totally acceptable, why are the courts virtually grid-locked with sexual harassment suits? Failure by the masses to treat sacred things with reverence does not legitimize the practice. Since this book is intended to help you avoid practices that weaken your relationship, consider the suggestions carefully before discarding them as old-fashioned or out-of-date.

There are special moments between husband and wife that do not include sex which would be better kept secret, special times when you have shared your innermost feelings and thoughts with each other. One needs violate those sacred trusts only once and the likelihood of a person sharing them with you a second time is remote.

Ironically, if you happen to allude to those private secrets between you, those are the very items that your friends will hound you incessantly to reveal to the group. It will require resolve and determination on both of your parts not to speak freely about those matters you have decided to keep private. Statements like: "What's the matter, don't you trust us?" or "If you were a real friend you'd share" are not uncommon. My response would be: "If you were are real friend, you won't ask me to break a confidence."

You will quickly discover that few people, even your very closest friends, can relate to your sacred experience as the two of you did. It is not that they are "dumb" or "insensitive" as much as that some things pass between people which are nonverbal communications. It would require the duplication of the entire environment (which is virtually impossible) to recreate the experience. Therefore, people often look at you like you have a screw loose when you try to explain something that the two of you have experienced.

Perhaps an example will illustrate this category of experiences. Some friends of ours claim to have had a very special experience at the birth of their mentally-handicapped child. In the labor room prior to giving birth, they said the baby, soon to be born, appeared to them in the form of a full-grown man. He smiled at them and nonverbally communicated his love and appreciation for the countless hours of sacrifice they would make in meeting his needs while he lived with them. It was a sacred, special moment for the two of them. The purpose of this recital is not to debate the reality of such an experience but to demonstrate a point. I was in a group of people where this couple shared the experience. Their sacred experience was met with disbelief by some, by snide remarks by others, and by outright rejection by still others. Although several people could feel their sincerity in sharing the experience, others could not. In retrospect, it would have saved them frustration and embarrassment if they had kept private that experience. If it indeed happened, it surely was intended for them and not for public consumption.

There is another group of experiences which may not be as sacred as they are embarrassing, which need to be kept secret unless mutually agreed to share. Those hilarious things that occasionally happen between couples which come to mean a great deal to the two of you but are only used by others to embarrass the person involved. Perhaps a single example will suffice to demonstrate the principle. I called a good friend a while ago in connection with a business dealing. His wife had been expecting a call from him and erroneously assumed that I was her husband. Instead of the traditional "hello," she seductively whispered into the phone "meow." I was rather taken back and said nothing. She must have realized her mistake immediately and said "hello." I could feel the embarrassment in her voice as she had mistakenly shared with me some intimate communication obviously intended for her husband. I teased her for a minute about it but soon determined that I would let that experience be a thing of the past. I am sure if I continued to use that mistake to taunt her, it would greatly weaken our friendship—something I would not want to happen.

If embarrassing things happen between the two of you (and they will inevitably happen!), be very careful to make sure both agree to share the experience **before** either of you share it. You have likely had a similar experience that I have witnessed many times over the years. It is usually a fun-filled party where husbands and wives are freely chatting about things they have experienced. It seems the intensity and intimacy of the shared experiences tend to escalate as the evening progresses. In an attempt to "match you and raise you one" one member of the couple starts to share a story which is private and usually embarrassing to the other. Quickly the other mate voices an objection and instructs the storyteller to stop. The crowd begins to encourage the storyteller to continue. The mate redoubles the warning to quit. The crowd wins and the story is told. The remainder of the evening is spent in total silence by the offended partner. A trust has been violated, a relationship has been weakened, and forgiveness will have to be sought or the marriage will lose a measure of love it had developed. All because something was shared that was private.

Often financial dealings are private in nature. Some couples are very open in discussing their financial dealings. If you disengage from the conversation long enough to stand as an outside observer, you may discover one of two reactions when financial matters are discussed by others. Either there is envy or disdain. If your financial situation is more secure than others, sharing your success story (although aggressively sought after and attentively listened to by the group) often results in you becoming an object of envy. Then, like a bucket of crabs which pull those trying to escape back into the bucket, some may begin to subtly plot your destruction. Even if nothing happens, you have put yourself in a position where the others in the group feel that you cannot identify with them in their more impoverished state, and so you are partially excluded from their group.

If you happen to be in the more financially-challenged group, others may see you as not very wise or creative financially because of your difficult circumstances. Again, you may find yourself being left out of the conversation because you may not be perceived as being as adept as the others in the group. The only difference between those who are included and those who are not may be how much the group knows about the financial dealings of the group. In many things in marriage, it is a safer course to err on the side of being too closed-mouth rather than blabbing everything you know. Stand back and observe the reaction of the group as others share their financial dealings. If it really is a mutually beneficial experience (and occasionally it is!) then this advice can carefully be disregarded. More often than not, you will discover that I am speaking from years of experience and the safer course is to keep private your financial dealings.

Some private things involve other people who are mutual acquaintances with the group. Sharing private knowledge with the group without the person being there is labeled "gossip." No one likes a gossip. Oh yes, often the gossip is the center of attention. People hang on their every word. However, when the latest "juicy" story has been shared and time has given the listeners a chance to think about the situation, you may find them turning away from you. Why? Because they are anything but sure that you won't do the same thing to them when they are not present. Hence, the very thing which makes you the center of attraction can also be the factor which eliminates you from having many close friends.

A philosopher once said: "Small minds talk about people, medium minds talk about things, but great minds talk about ideas." The saying sort of stuck with me although I have forgotten who said it. I didn't want to be labeled as having either a small or medium mind so I started talking about ideas with my friends. At first they looked at me like I was trying to be some intellectual. Then they discovered that some of their most mind-expanding experiences followed our conversations. Before long our social experiences changed from being gossip sessions to idea- generating experiences. Several of our friends attribute new business ideas to the discussion of ideas during our get-togethers. One friend, a multi-millionaire, said, "Lock three men of average intelligence in a room for an hour with an assignment to brainstorm about ideas for businesses, and in an hour they will have come up with at least a dozen ideas which, if implemented, would easily make each of them a millionaire." I wonder if we miss some golden opportunities because we have fallen into the habit of wasting our valuable time and mental energy engaging in conversations which only weaken friendly relationships?

Finally there are personal problems which have been shared with the two of you but were not intended to be public information. When others value your opinion and friendship enough to share private parts of their lives with you, you must safeguard those confidences with your life. I can think of no higher compliment than to have someone trust me enough to share a confidence with me. Since knowledge is power, there is a real temptation to share what you know with other people. If you violate that confidence just once, you will likely never earn that trust back again. It is always an amazement when something that I have known for years finally becomes public knowledge and I confess that I have known that for a long time. I usually don't inform people in a boasting or gloating way about my prior knowledge, but say something like, "I have known that for some time now."

Without focusing the attention on my ability to keep a secret, others have silently noted that I can be trusted to keep a secret. Perhaps that is why so many people feel confident that they can share private things with me without the fear of it becoming public knowledge. I have many friends who have perfected the art of keeping secrets. They are so much more valued than those who, when told something, can hardly wait to make it known to others.

Some people call the talkers "the underground." In a large company or among a group of friends, I find it almost a game to discover who is on the "underground" and how to use them. The game is that I will drop several different bits of information to several different people and then watch to see how quickly and how accurately the privileged information gets back to me. It only takes a little while before you know who can be trusted and who can't. I have found that some people are faster than the Postal Service in getting the message out—and they are much cheaper. Unfortunately, they have a reputation I am sure you would not like to have.

Far superior to having people find out that you cannot be trusted with private information is to have enough integrity to know what information needs to be kept private and then the stability of character sufficient to keep quiet. There is a certain self-confidence when a person realizes that he or she can be trusted. In marriage that trust is crucial to building a stable foundation. As a friend you are invaluable because of your almost unique ability to keep a secret. If you have had a problem in the past with sharing private information, isn't now a good time to get started on the right track?

12

SEEKING PROFESSIONAL HELP WHEN PROBLEMS GET THE UPPER HAND

— ♥ —

Occasionally, in spite of our best preventative efforts, the invading armies of germs overcome our immune system and we become ill. At those times wisdom dictates that we make an appointment to see a doctor. No one cries "wimp" or "sissy" when we go to the emergency room to have a doctor examine us to determine the cause of the severe pain in our lower abdomen. Why would it be any different for marital problems which overcome our best preventative methods?

Lest we understate the obvious—life is full of problems. Problems do not signal either failure or defeat. Properly viewed and attacked, problems become a source of growth in our marriage. It isn't in the having of problems that we make our greatest mistakes, it is often the methodology we employ to solve them which is often flawed.

A close friend of ours had a severe stuttering problem. He made miraculous improvement when he linked up with a speech pathologist—an expert. If you are having trouble communicating in marriage, couldn't a professional give you some guidance that may result in the same degree of miraculous improvement as with our stuttering friend? It would be silly not to use all resources available to achieve maximum progress with minimum expense. Isn't that our goal in all areas of life? The most for the least.

Since finances are usually a major concern during the early years of marriage, you may feel you don't have the funds necessary to see a marriage counselor. Two points: (1) if your problems are severe enough that your marriage may not survive without counseling, you can't afford **not** to go! and (2) there are other "para-professionals" available who may be just as proficient as the high-paid professional in helping you solve your problems, who are willing to give you advice for free.

There are counselors by profession and then there are counselors who are naturals. You may even be a natural counselor. You'll recognize that you have that talent if people seek you out for advice in solving their problems. You may have a favorite aunt or an older fellow down the street, or, a minister or any of a dozen other people who can help you see the answer to your problem more clearly. If you have confidence in their ability to help you, chances are they will be all that is necessary.

As with so many other issues mentioned in this book, make sure you both agree that you need help and where you turn for that help. If your mate does not see the need for external help, you can get some help, but the problems will not be solved until you tackle them together. It would not be wise nor growth producing to hastily set an appointment to see a counselor at the very first sign of a problem. As mentioned above, solving problems can be very beneficial in helping you learn sound principles that will bless your lives forever. However, there is a point of diminishing returns. After so many abortive tries at problem-solving, it may not be productive to continue knocking your head against the same wall—it will only result in a more severe headache.

Assuming that you have tried every conceivable approach you both can think of to solve the problem and nothing has worked, go together to see the counselor. Agree to try the counsel given. The best medicine does absolutely no good unless you take it. The best counsel, which would immediately make an observable difference in your situation, will do absolutely no good if it falls on deaf ears. My suggested motto here is "Adopt before you adapt." Too many couples who have returned for follow up visits admit that they didn't fully agree with what I had recommended so they altered it. Often the very key element to the successful change in their marriage is the very part they altered. If your philosophy for solving the problem was not flawed, you wouldn't be seeing a counselor in the first place. Place some trust in the recommendations given and see if they work—even if they differ from your personal beliefs.

Since communication problems are the root of almost all other problems in marriage (and in life!), it seems important to emphasize the point. Learning how to talk rather than just chat is essential. Before marriage you may have chattered like canaries. Now the issues are much heavier and more important and you may feel at a loss not knowing how to express yourself. Parents are often more than willing to help you solve your problems. A strong caution should be given. Parents often tend to "take sides" in the battle. Almost exclusively, they favor their child. Therefore the counsel they give may be jaded. Make sure you agree to consult your parents and then be doubly sure to stand back and weigh their counsel for possible prejudice. Having stated that caution, let's proceed.

Parents are often a great source of help. They may be able to throw tremendous light on why one or the other of you act or think the way you do. It was a real revelation to me when my grandmother confided that my great-grandfather was the sulking type. Although that revelation came before we were married, that was the point where I realized that our family had a tradition to break. Had grandmother not shared that with me, I may have thought that sulking was just another acceptable way of solving problems.

Be careful not to use "that's the way his father is too" as an excuse for unacceptable behavior. Bad habits can and should be broken. No amount of family tradition is worth the destroying of a marriage. The earlier in your marriage you can identify the potentially explosive traditional family problems, the easier it is to take evasive action.

Friends are often not the best people to discuss your problems with. They lack the wisdom which comes with age. Their experiences have been very minimal and therefore what worked once for them, may very well blow up in their faces the next time they try it. Friends are not always "true friends." Many people turn out to be "fair weather friends." In other words, as long as everything is going well, they stand by you. When things get tough they may harbor a secret desire to see you fail. If they are secretly envious of your marriage and success, they may say all the right words but their intentions are more sinister. Somehow they think that your looking bad will make them look better. Turn to the tried and proven friends.

Of course many of your friends can give you encouragement and some very good advice. It stands to reason that those enduring the trials will have some good ideas that may be helpful as you try to work through your challenges. What I would suggest is that you seek counsel from others who are not your peers. See if the counsel is the same or parallels the counsel of your friends. Then be very careful if the young direct you in paths divergent from those who are tried and seasoned. Use friends as "a" source of counsel, not as "the" sole source of counsel.

Clergy may offer some sound advice. If you have confidence in your clergyman, he may be able to draw upon his or her knowledge of the scriptures to bring more light to bear on how the Lord would suggest you attack the problem. Don't be too disappointed if your clergyman does not draw the relationship between what he teaches every Sunday and how we live our lives every day. I have found that not everyone can take a sermon and make it relevant to my daily challenges.

Before entrusting your problems to an expert, look at his or her credentials. Can they apply their own advice? It would be ridiculous to choose your financial counselor from those exiting a bankruptcy court. If a person's marriage has fallen apart, he or she may be able to tell you what not to do, but that does not automatically mean that they can tell you how to succeed. Look, rather, to those who are successfully negotiating the storms of life.

If at all possible, talk with someone who has counseled with the proposed counselor you are considering. What was their experience? Did they feel they were given good, functional direction? Were their charges fair and reasonable? Did they terminate the counseling when the problem was remedied or did they keep inviting you back thus escalating the cost? These are the kinds of questions to investigate.

Everyone has read about or heard of professionals who are unscrupulous. They are few and far between but they can give the whole profession a black eye. Because there are some unethical counselors out there, it pays you big dividends to find out who they are and avoid them like a plague. Perhaps someday the self-governing mechanisms in each profession will work as they are intended. Until then, it would be helpful to keep a cautious eye out.

Sharing your financial challenges with too many people is not a wise move. Contrary to what you may perceive, almost every newly-married couple has troubles adjusting. One of the curses of mankind when not properly controlled is "plastic money." In a later chapter we will deal directly with the problem. Here we mention it merely to alert you that there are experts (again some are trained professional money managers and others are just naturally good at handling money) who are more than willing to teach you some sound financial principles.

Probably more than in other professions, there are unscrupulous people who prey on the young and inexperienced. The trigger raising the cautionary flags in this area should be more sensitive than in almost any other area. If a person stands to profit from you financially, be cautious about their counsel. If they are successful themselves and do not have a profit motive in the suggestions they give you, you may proceed with less caution. For example, the advice you receive from your parents or trusted older friend concerning the amount of insurance you need, would probably be more realistic than a commission-hungry insurance salesperson.

One more word of advice concerning financial counselors, in the early days of your marriage, why not seek advice from those who are older, stable, but not so affluent? The rich are apt to give advice which you cannot afford. Those who are "making it" but do not have money to burn are often best at giving conservative advice.

Another area where seeking the help of professionals (both trained and natural) might be advisable, is raising children. It would be impossible to keep your children on ice long enough for you to learn all the lessons people have learned by their experience. As you observe families interacting, you will rapidly discern that some families run smoothly and others need some serious, immediate engine work. While it is instructive to make a list of those experiences you want your family to avoid, it isn't as easy to identify those qualities you want to incorporate. Most people can identify a dysfunctional family. It is far more difficult to isolate those factors contributing to the success of a marriage and family.

Taking classes through the community college may be helpful. There are television programs which may give you some ideas. But the best advice may come from those who have similar backgrounds and are seasoned by the rearing of their own children. Parents, grandparents, uncles, aunts, elderly friends, all are willing to share the "tricks of the trade" with you. Don't be afraid to ask, but weigh their advice carefully before you implement it. It might be helpful to ask your aged friends a question like: "What did your parents do right in raising you?" or "What do you wish your parents had done differently while raising you?" They are less likely to be protective of errors that were made. In considering my response when asked how we have done it successfully, I tend to emphasize the good things we do and minimize the mistakes we've made. By removing your inquiry by one generation, the reluctance to talk about what should have happened will be eliminated. I find that in talking about what I wished my parents had done differently, I incorporate more easily many of the mistakes we have made.

If you are really struggling sexually, be very cautious about turning to the world for ideas leading to success. It appears from their obsessive focus on the subject that they should be experts. However, their track record is similar to their divorce rate—dismal. I would recommend that you contact a competent medical doctor for advice. Unless you have a really progressive set of parents, their ideas (and their willingness to talk openly with you!) may be somewhat dated. Generally speaking, newly married couples do not have too much trouble figuring out how things are to work. It is in the aberrations and perversions that problems arise. Talking with those who have no basis other than their own personal experience, may not bear as many fruits as you would desire.

As life passes, there are transitional challenges which must be made. The first year tends to pose the greatest number of these challenges. You are welding two entirely different personalities, families, backgrounds, and often cultures into a single unit. There are bound to be problems to be overcome.

Transitions from being single to being married are seemingly without number. Learning to be considerate of your mate after either having lived alone for so many years or having lived in a family setting where your parents performed many of the essential, mundane tasks may be extremely challenging. This entire book deals with transitional changes which the newly married must make.

There is also the transition from being married to having children, from being in school to entering the work force, from living near parents and families to moving to a distant city, from joining long established family traditions to starting traditions of your own. You can get a glimpse of the magnitude of the transitions facing you from what I have mentioned. If you stop to catalog the changes, you may be overwhelmed. Thankfully, they happen just one day at a time and many can even be postponed (temporarily!) if you are not up to making the decisions now. Eventually, however, you will want to establish your own lives by addressing these transitional changes.

Change is often difficult although it does not have to be something to be avoided. As you face these transitions, the best professionals to consult are those who have successfully made the transitions themselves. I felt particularly sensitive towards a young woman from South Carolina who is taking a class from me. She seemed a little down one day so I asked if everything was all right. She started to cry and said everything should be wonderful since she just became engaged to a fine young man. However, it dawned on her that they would live on the opposite side of the country from her family. She was already missing being close to her father. I knew exactly how she felt having moved to North Carolina when we were first married. A word of encouragement from one who had walked that path before was all she needed to reassure her that she wasn't making a terrible mistake. We talked for a few minutes about methods of keeping close to family even when geographically separated by great distances. As her vision expanded, the ungrounded fears began to evaporate. It really seemed important to her to talk to someone who had "been there, done that" and survived.

Contrary to the way you may feel, almost everyone in the aging generation has had to face transitional changes similar to yours. Some have very successfully made those changes and some have resisted to the point of absurdity. Seeking counsel on how to lessen the pain of transitions is not a sign of weakness or cowardice.

Perhaps we have taken enough time to consider turning to the experts. One final question is worth asking: "what constitutes an expert?" Does going to school for a certain number of years automatically make a person an expert? Does the fact that a person has never been to school to specialize in a given field disqualify them as being an expert? Hopefully, you can see where I am going. An expert is one who has entered the battle and successfully emerged as the victor. Unfortunately, we do not have access to those who have completed the entire obstacle course of life—they are dead! But we do have those who have emerged from the fog of different battlefields and can urge us on with their example and words. They have made it and so can we.

We need to exercise supreme caution about taking direction from those who have failed the test and yet profess to be experts. We also need to be cautious about holding in too high esteem the advice of those who are still in the midst of the battle. They may very well emerge as the next generation of true experts. They may just as well never emerge at all. Someone must be wise enough to recognize the gold medalists as the winners—not just the participants.

13

AGREEING TO DISAGREE WITHOUT BEING DISAGREEABLE

— ♥ —

In Chapter 8 we talked about solving problems without arguing. There we discussed some techniques of resolving differences by eliminating "unknowns." Other suggestions focused on working around conflicting wants. In this chapter we will deal with the attitudes and methods of disagreeing and still staying in love and not becoming so offensive no one wants to associate with you.

Differences will arise. It seems virtually impossible to weld two individuals into one, realizing that they come from different backgrounds, without some disagreement. Starting from one of our frequently stated foundations: Establish, before marriage if possible, and if not, as soon after as possible, the ground rule that you will treat each other civilly. If you ignore this foundational stone, the very basis of your marriage is compromised. In the early days of our courtship, we stated it this way: "If we are old enough to get married, we are old enough to act like adults even when things go wrong or when we disagree." Little children throw temper tantrums, fight and scratch, or sulk. Adults should have grown out of childish ways. Far too many adults still employ childish behavior when confronted with an innocent, honest difference in marriage.

Is it possible to control your response to the surprises of life at all times? Consider how controlled you are at work even when the walls fall in around you. Seldom, if ever, do you throw a tantrum or lose your temper or verbally assassinate a colleague—especially if that person is in a power position over you. It isn't that circumstances never warrant such a reaction. It is that the consequences of such uncontrolled behavior would have such negative repercussions that you suppress the inclination to act out your frustrations.

Considering the long-term, far reaching possible implications of uncontrolled behavior in marriage, it seems only logical that the greater the self-restraint, the more likely success in marriage would be. Assuming that you both agree that controlling the response is desirable and something to be perfected, let us turn our attention to some methods of control.

While I was growing up, I learned the truth of the biblical proverb: "A soft answer turneth away wrath: but grievous words stir up anger" (Proverbs 15:1). Of course, in those early days, I was more prone to learn by sad experience than by being taught. My older brother who was six inches taller and outweighed me by fifty pounds helped me learn a valuable lesson. It is often better to keep my mouth shut until I weighed the possible results of my answer than to speak my mind and spend the next few days trying to physically recover. As a married man I have learned that my wife has very acute hearing so there really isn't a physical need to raise my voice, even when discussing the most emotional, controversial topics.

Often the resistance to your point of view will be directly proportional to the level of your voice. I find that especially true with our children. The more softly I speak, the more likely they are to conform without resistance. It seems a truism that loudness violates almost every principle upon which this book is built. In dealing with each other, resolve now **never** to raise your voice at each other. The only possible exceptions should be when your mate's life is in imminent danger and you need to alert them to the danger.

Avoid the "in your face" syndrome. When you want to make a point, it is easier for your companion to be far enough away so their eyes can focus. I have watched in wonderment as a couple stood nose to nose in the grocery store, yelling at each other so loudly that I questioned their need for hearing aids. They were so close that neither could see more than the angry eyes of their mate and certainly the sharing of the bad breath only exaggerated the problem. How childish! They did accomplish one thing—they made everyone in the store a party to their disagreement. I'm sure they were totally unaware of their being the negative focal point of the entire establishment. They definitely were in a lose-lose situation. I left before they concluded their argument. I exited renewing my resolve never to try solving problems by using force or loud language.

Make it a point to stay a comfortable social distance away even when you are trying to emphasize your point. Putting your finger in someone's face only adds another anger-producing gesture to an already potentially explosive situation. Reverse the situation. How would you like your boss at work or anyone else yelling at you and menacingly pointing at you? If you would not enjoy that kind of confrontation, then don't do it yourself.

Don't use "fightin'words." You know the words that tend to make a person angry. The following verse in the quotation from Proverbs sheds more light on Solomon's wisdom: "The tongue of the wise useth knowledge aright: but the mouth of fools poureth out foolishness" (Proverbs 15:2). Sometimes it is the poor choice of words which exacerbates the situation. Accusatory words, phrases which diminish a person's self-worth, or cast a negative light on their intelligence never produce positive results. We have all had enough experience "picking fights" by the things we say or the way we say them. Why not focus on the more difficult task of defusing the explosive situation?

As you grow together you will discover that the way you say things is often more effective in communicating your intent than the actual words themselves. Make sure that the way you say things confirms your words and doesn't contradict them. For example, the phrase, "Oh, that was really smart!" said with genuine intent can be a real compliment. Said in a sarcastic tone of voice, those same words crush and destroy self-esteem.

Once you have let words fly from your mouth, they are impossible to recall. It is better to be a little slow responding than to always employ the quick response and almost immediately regretting it. Take a few seconds to formulate your response so your mate will not only understand what you intend, but so that he or she cannot misunderstand. We seem to live in a time in which silence (even momentary) is misconstrued as a negative. Pausing a few seconds to collect your thoughts gives both parties the opportunity to rethink their stance. Some issues are so silly that they really don't even merit discussion. When you find yourself in one of those conversations which leads nowhere and has no real merit, be big enough to stop and restart the conversation in a more productive direction. A simple "I just said a dumb thing. Let me start all over" can back you out of a dead-ended verbal road that goes nowhere.

There are ways of saying things which are annoying. Just because your folks always talked that way does not make it right. If your mate is irritated by some gesture or way of saying things, let your love and concern for them override your need to use that technique. Any method you employ which is manipulative, condescending, or intimidating is counterproductive to a solid marriage.

Can you disagree even with a great degree of emotion without being disagreeable? The answer is "Yes." The qualifier is, "It takes a lot of practice on your part and patience on your mate's part." Being definite or even emotional does not signalize an argument or fight as long as you are focusing on the issue in question. When the emotion is directed towards your mate, then you are rapidly slipping into forbidden territory.

If, during your establishing phase, you both agree to address the issues where you differ, you will discover that it is less likely to be viewed as a flaw in your marriage when differences are confronted. If your vision of marriage is that you will always agree on every issue, you will likely see your differences as marriage threatening.

Agreeing to disagree is an important concept. There may be some issues where total agreement is not possible. For example, my wife loves pizza. On the other hand, I hate pizza. We have just agreed to disagree. I don't mock her for eating it and she has graciously agreed to fry me a hamburger when they have pizza. It isn't a big issue unless you insist on making it such. She will likely never convert me to liking pizza and chances are better than average I will never convince her not to eat it. We still love each other and find that our disagreement is not significant. If the issues were more vital to our happiness, it could cause additional stress unless we were willing to devise a fair method of compromise.

On some issues there isn't much room for compromise. For example, if you feel that spanking is an acceptable means of disciplining children and your mate is horrified at the thought, there isn't much room for compromise. You cannot both spank and not spank a child. There is little or no compromise when your mate does not want children and you want them or vice versa. Hopefully, you talked these major issues through before you got married. Otherwise, these, and many other similar issues put so much strain on your new marriage, that serious problems may arise.

Laughter is a wonderful salve in marriage. Laughter can destroy marriages! The obvious difference is the timing and the "meta-message" (i.e. unspoken message sent by the tone and body language) conveyed. Sometimes when the discussion has become ludicrous, a good laugh between you is therapeutic. Sometimes, laughing when your mate is trying to seriously resolve a difference can hurt and destroy tender feelings. It doesn't require a doctor's degree in psychology to know when it is appropriate to laugh and when it is not. It may require a PhD in self-restraint to resist the temptation to make light of a serious topic at an inappropriate time.

Some of the most frustrating people I know and am constrained to work around are those who do not know how to adapt their behavior to the appropriateness of the situation. They are still trying to be funny when it is time to get serious. They are trying to be serious after the decision is made and the party has begun. They want to discuss weighty matters at a social gathering. The list goes endlessly on. I think you know the type. I'm not sure how to help them develop some social sensitivity, but a sensitive mate can do wonders for them.

Sometimes the disagreements are genuine. Other times, people are disagreeable just to be disagreeable. I remember being at a party where two options were presented as possible activities for the night. A vote was taken. One fellow abstained from voting when his turn came to give everyone else a chance to express themselves. I thought (initially) that he had made a gentlemanly gesture. However, after the discussion was over and everyone had agreed on which option to take, he stepped up and voted for the other option. Then I could see that he was a spoiler. It didn't really make that much difference to him what we did. He just wanted to be contrary. He could have joined in on the discussion and expressed his point of view along with the others. He chose to make everyone uncomfortable by being disagreeable.

If you have inclinations to be a spoiler, think twice before you act. You may gain some very short-lived satisfaction from disrupting the party and feelings of harmony, but you will lose big time in the long run. Before long you will find that you are excluded from the party or given the label of being a "party pooper" or ignored altogether. It isn't fair to your mate who will suffer along with you for your insensitivity. In marriage there are few things that weaken the relationship faster than being a spoiler. It is almost impossible to envision a marriage staying together when one partner is constantly trying to sabotage the plans and activities of the rest.

If you are going to make a significant contribution to your marriage, you must learn to be a team player. That entails more than always having things your way. As you sense the joy that comes from going along with the crowd on issues that don't make that much difference, you will rapidly discard any inclinations you have to breed contention and division among the group.

A person who can unify a marriage, a family, or a group, will find themselves in high demand whenever people get together. A person who can take a divided group and find the common threads and help them come to a unity of the minds can almost write his own ticket through life. Anyone can be divisive. It takes a person with keen intellect and a lot of social skills to bring harmony and unity. Practicing the art of unifying will not only enrich your marriage, but will also increase your worth in the social world. What would happen on the international front if we had leaders who had mastered the skills of unifying instead of dividing?

If you are really in touch with yourself and your mate, you may discover that there are certain times of the day or month during which disagreements are more likely. For instance, many women report that at certain times during their monthly menstrual cycle, they are more combative, more moody, more argumentative than during the rest of the month. It is wise to identify those times and avoid discussing controversial issues during those times. Continue that practice until those fluctuating emotions can be controlled even though the inclinations may still be there. In addition, many couples realize that late at night is a sorry time to address potentially-explosive topics. A smile, a kiss, and an agreed postponement can avoid the marriage weakening argument which frequently occurs when you insist on discussing the matter at the wrong time.

There are also other times when you are more apt to be disagreeable. After a bad day at work or with the kids, you may unconsciously be looking for someone to vent your frustrations on. When you are experiencing a sugar-low you may sense that you are more sullen, sulky, or difficult to reason with. Avoid those times by doing something to remedy the problem—eat a candy bar, drink some juice, or whatever works for you.

You may discover yourself in "one of those moods" for no apparent reason at all. Just because you don't understand why you're in a bad mood does not mean you aren't in a bad mood. Learning to be totally honest with yourself and each other can avoid ninety percent of the disagreeable confrontations couples usually experience.

As you both mature, you may discover that consciously talking yourself out of a combative mood is very do-able. If you can completely alter your mood between the time the phone rings and the time you answer it, why can't you alter your mood even when the phone does not ring? What a powerful message we send our spouse when we are willing to change into a good mood for some unknown person on the telephone and are unwilling to snap out of our bad mood for the person we love the very most—our spouse.

You may find that there are certain topics upon which agreement is not possible and which usually are highly emotionally charged. Agree to leave them alone. Whether the difference is over a relative who is loved by one and detested by the other, or over a particular activity attractive to one and repugnant to the other, you will know what they are. They inevitably result in strained relationships and hard feelings. The problems are generally magnified because they are brought up when one or both of you are in a combative mood. This is where your maturity is tested to the max. Are you really adult enough to agree to leave the issue alone until you are in a more conciliatory mood? If not, you are embarking on the path to a serious marital battle.

Very often politics, either parties or issues, lend themselves to emotional disagreements. There is seldom a "right" or "wrong" choice to be made. It generally is a "wise" or "not-so-wise" choice our leaders must make. Unfortunately we seldom have enough absolute true information to make an informed decision. Therefore we argue over that which we know little or nothing about or that which we have a view in a distorted light because of misinformation.

Athletic allegiances often generate fertile seed beds for disagreement. Especially is this true if you graduated from rival high schools or colleges. There needs to come a time in life when we are willing to allow high school and college rivalries to die. Marriage is far too important to sacrifice it on the football field or basketball court. If you discover that you have trouble staying reasonable when discussing sports—be wise enough to discuss something else.

When you distance yourself from daily living, you discover that virtually everything has the potential of being a point of conflict. Therefore, it is not only desirable but absolutely imperative that couples learn how to disagree without being disagreeable. Practice in this area will prove invaluable. It is impossible to avoid areas of potential conflict since that would result in our constantly avoiding each other. Therefore, in summary, there are things that are in our best interest to avoid because they always result in hard feelings. There are many other issues upon which we will disagree, but agree not to become adversarial just because a consensus can not be (or has not yet been) achieved. There are many times when we will disagree vehemently but do not need to be disagreeable in our methods. Many of the disagreements can and should be eliminated by talking them through before the wedding or as soon afterwards as possible. Working for harmony and love in a marriage will greatly enhance your ability to disagree without being disagreeable.

14

BUILDING ON THE COMMON

— ♥ —

It is a constant amazement to me to sit in a busy mall or airport and watch people pass by on their way to a million different destinations. Have you ever noticed how unique each person is? Even when identical twins are observed over a period of time, there are obvious differences. We all readily agree that we are different, then why in marriage do we tend to focus on those differences rather than trying to find the areas of common interest? Life would probably be pretty dull if everyone were a carbon copy of everyone else. The next chapter will deal with differences and how to maximize them. However, in this chapter we want to focus on what we have in common.

When you first started dating, what attracted you to each other? Of the millions of people we pass each year, we are only attracted to a very small number. Could it be that each person radiates certain "vibes" or feelings which attract people who have similar feelings? Since I teach on the university level and it is in that environment that many young people find their mates, I am frequently asked how to find the "right one." Over the years I have come to the conclusion that it is easier to "be" the right one and radiate those characteristics you want in a mate and then let that magnetism occur naturally.

If you would like a case study to work on, try determining why you are attracted to one person and not to another. Good looks may have something to do with it, but you will soon discover that there is much more to an affectionate relationship than looks. If there isn't, you are in serious trouble when age begins to diminish your desirability based solely on looks.

In the scientific world the opposite poles of a magnet attract. In fact, if you attempt to force common poles together, they repel to the strength of the magnet. In the social arena, likes attract. Those who have an athletic bent are attracted to those with similar interests. Those who major in academic pursuits often pair up with those of similar I.Q.'s. Those who are attracted to the outdoors often date and marry those who love camping and hiking. The list is virtually endless. The trick is to find a person who has a sufficient number of similar interests so that you have a broad base for your friendship.

If you both like movies and that is the extent of your similarities, your relationship could be in serious trouble before you even get started. It does not seem possible (nor desirable) to be perfectly matched. As you date, you may discover that in order to insure adequate stability, you need to develop more areas of commonalities. As you share in each other's worlds and desire to spend more time together, you may broaden each other's circles of interests. This in turn may increase the number of things you love doing with your mate. During the honeymoon, you are so wound up in each other that you become almost oblivious to the world around you. That is a temporary state and not one that should be expected to last forever. After coming home from the honeymoon, couples begin to reestablish their own worlds. Jobs have to be attended to, homes or apartments established, friendships renewed, etc. Unless you both are careful, your worlds begin to separate again. It isn't usually a catastrophic event but rather a gradual, global drift. If you do not do something to curb the separation of your worlds, you may find that you are two people living under the same roof with very little in common.

Like you, I know people who are virtual strangers living under the same roof and married—at least the law says so. They are unhappy and seem ignorant of the reasons. The love that propelled them to marriage has diminished until neither is sure that it is still there. Can you sense the frustration such a situation would cause? As couples in that deplorable state come in to see me, I suggest that they start courting again. Start doing the things which caused them to fall in love in the first place. Start broadening their circle of interests and begin again including each other in that circle. Stop resisting the trying of new things calculated to reintroduce each other into your own little world circle.

The number of couples who will take the challenge to re-include each other in their circle have almost a 100% success rate in rekindling their lost love. Those who refuse to give it a try claiming that it wouldn't do any good and they really don't have the desire to try, have almost an identical percentage rate of failure. Without common ground, it is nearly impossible to hold a marriage together with any degree of joy and satisfaction.

If you stay vigilant, you need never get to the "strangers under the same roof" state. From the onset of your marriage, be aware that love, like a campfire, needs to be fed and fanned. A weekly date night, alternating who selects the activity, is usually sufficient to keep life interesting. More will be suggested in a later chapter about how to keep the courtship alive.

In watching international peace negotiations over the years, I have noticed a trend. When time is taken to identify the points of common interest or common goals, the negotiations go much better and the result is always more positive. If focus is initially given to their differences and incompatible goals, the peace talks tend to break down or end without favorable progress. Often the most productive summit meetings are held on neutral grounds and moderated by a third party.

Capitalizing on some of those points may prove helpful in marriage. Start "fixing" your marriage by focusing on what is happening that is right and good. That is very therapeutic because in order to find the common and good one, must look for it. When you start to look for the good in your relationship, it soon becomes apparent that there is much there to be found. When all you do is look for the negative, that too is very easy to find. You will likely find whatever you look for. That is true in life as well as in marriage. Why can one assembly line worker be so happy and content while the worker at his or her elbow is constantly complaining and miserable? Could it be that we find in life exactly what we look for?

When the normal challenges of marriage begin, unless you are focusing on the good and the positive, you become more aware of the areas of friction. Make a mental list of the areas of common interest so that when difficult days come, you may sustain the interest in your marriage by engaging together in those areas you both like. Even if you are straining to keep a conversation going, you might find it easier when you go to the zoo or a park or a ball game or an opera or whatever you both enjoy doing. When you return to environments where you enjoyed easy conversation before your marriage, it is more conducive to re-instituting conversation when it is more difficult to communicate.

Joint projects often require cooperation and communication to accomplish. If you both enjoy woodworking (for example) and want to make something for a favorite aunt or uncle for Christmas, many enjoyable hours can be spent together working in close proximity to finish your mutual goal by a given deadline. Gardening is another project many couples enjoy. If you take the time to identify the projects while you are still in the honeymoon part of your relationship, it is easy to find something to reunite you later on. Conversation during those long hours together almost becomes a natural activity. Before long the strained, superficial topics are depleted and real meaningful discussions take place.

Super-ordinate tasks (those which the two of you can accomplish working together but which neither of you can successfully complete alone) are great unifiers. In the army multimillions of dollars are spent to construct obstacle courses which require recruits to work as a team to successfully complete the tasks. The army understands the essential need of unity when sending soldiers into combat. The same is true of marriage. Even something so simple as holding a board or piece of sheet rock in place while the other secures it with nails requires cooperation. If you carefully consider life, most of what we do is "super-ordinate." Even if you do not work together as husband and wife, you will find that either the husband or the wife will have to turn elsewhere to complete many of the things we do each day. Why not stay focused on each other?

Whenever couples come in for counseling I ask them to detail the areas of conflict and also the times when conflict is most likely to occur. They usually talk about several areas of conflict but, ironically, the times of the conflicts are relatively few. I ask about the other twenty-two or twenty-three hours a day when they are not fighting. Usually they say that they are apart during working hours, sleeping during some of the time and they get along all right during the rest of the time. When we do an analysis, invariably they are surprised to note that they get along for a much greater portion of the day than the time they spend disagreeing.

As you separate yourself from the emotion of the disagreeable situation, you begin to analyze and evaluate the differences between when you argue and when you get along. There may be certain hours of the day when you are both tired and irritable when it would be better to agree not to discuss anything volatile. Most of the serious arguments I mediate with warring couples are not issues that must be solved "right now." We are generally much more congenial when we are rested, when our stomachs are full, and when the pressure of deadlines is not looming over our heads. Be reasonable enough to recognize the warning flags of potential marital explosions and take steps to avoid such situations.

In suggesting that you agree to disengage before problems erupt, I am not saying that there isn't a time when you confront the unresolved issues. This entire book is founded on identifying the problems and solving them. But it would be foolish, to say the least, to walk across an open field during a lightning storm dressed in your coat of armor when you have the option of waiting until the storm has passed.

Long before the wedding, set goals together. Dream together and make plans together. All of these activities contribute to areas of commonality where you can retreat in times of trouble. If you are struggling to get started with your planning sessions or dream sessions, talk to others who seem to be having success at their efforts in building a successful marriage.

As you enter into your marital relationship, be cautious about taking advice from those who are not experiencing success themselves. It is always easier to tell others how to be happy than it is to live in the way of happiness yourself. Even if you disagree with the way other couples make decisions, plan activities, discipline their children, etc., if you envy the happiness and harmony they enjoy, try to figure out how they accomplish it and try to implement those things in your marriage. In other words, don't discard a couple as potential role models just because there are portions of their relationship you do not agree with. You can selectively take that which is good and leave the rest out of your relationship.

Building on the common in marriage is like going to a supermarket or a department store. If you only frequent the corner market in a small town, you may discover that the variety is very limited thus curtailing your choices. In a large store you may choose from many different brands of the same item. Unless you continually look for and broaden the choices in marriage, you may find the items available are old, stale, and not very appealing. Watch people, talk with other couples, read books, watch movies, experiment on new and unusual things yourselves and then you'll more likely have a greater resource pool from which to choose your next activity.

The final point I would like to emphasize in this chapter is the absolute necessity of building on the foundation of common beliefs. You may not think religion is very important in your life and to this point you may be right. But consider the backgrounds of your individual families. Are either of your families religiously oriented? Are they very different from each other in their orientation? Have you discussed your feelings about going to church, baptism of your children, your attitude towards the scriptures and prayer?

Often the true feelings about spirituality and one's relationship to God are not clearly defined until some of the crises of life crash in around you. When a child is terminally ill, when a close relative is injured or killed in an accident, when a parent is diagnosed with cancer, when a major financial set-back occurs, then we start to ask for a broader understanding of life and why these things happen. Even if your families are drastically different, you can decide between the two of you how you want your marriage to be spiritually focused. If you choose to take the road where God is included, then you should both agree to look in that direction when the problems occur. The divisiveness comes when one of you turns to God and the other refused to follow suit.

If you establish common spiritual ground before the marriage, the direction you take as young married couples will not add to the problems you are experiencing. Many young couples choose a church to attend together and virtually start their own legacy of spirituality even though neither family has instilled religious traditions in their lives. It may be something both of you determine is the direction you want to go. Establishing those spiritual patterns early in your relationship helps create good habits that are easier to maintain during difficult times.

It is with spirituality as with every other factor in marriage, the more common ground you can establish early in your marriage, the less likely that you will suffer any marriage threatening problems later on. Take the time to identify that which you have in common. If you are lacking or limited, expend the energy to create common ground. If you sense that there is more you can do to broaden your common ground, do whatever is necessary so that there is never a time when you become strangers living under the same roof.

15

RECOGNIZING BEAUTY AND STRENGTH IN DIVERSITY

— ♥ —

Having discussed the necessity of building on common ground, it is now necessary that we turn our attention to rounding out the concept of how to successfully build on our differences. We have already noted that we are different and distinct individuals. Are we to try to eliminate the differences in order to insure a stable marriage? Certainly not! Only those who are so insecure in who they are and the strengths they have will consider it even desirable to change others into becoming like themselves.

When you do your financial analysis before marriage, you take inventory of what resources (both positive and negative) both of you will bring to the relationship. How much money will be available to you? When can you expect to receive that income? Will it be monthly, biweekly, weekly? What are the fixed bills that will come due every month? Every six months? Every year? What debts will each partner bring into marriage? How will they be paid? What is the remaining balance? Questions like these will help the couple paint an accurate picture of how their financial future looks.

Equally as important as an accurate financial picture (perhaps, infinitely more important) is to do an inventory of nonmaterial resources each partner is bringing to the relationship. I have always worked well with numbers. Balancing the checkbook, for me, is something I enjoy doing and could do it when I'm half asleep. My wife, on the other hand, had a really bad experience during a high school math class and consequently has hated working with numbers ever since. She has a mental block which seems to make it impossible for her to balance the checkbook. No problem, I have the talent to perform that vital function. Can you see the point? It isn't crucial that both members of the marriage have identical talents. One is sufficient.

My wife is very creative. She can paint pictures that are incredible. She has a difficult time understanding why my pictures resemble a first grader's work. I can not understand how anyone can take a blank canvas and create a masterpiece. Just because I cannot paint does not make me less of a person. I have talents in other areas. If we want something painted in our family, even the smallest child knows better than to ask me for help. They make a beeline straight to mom.

If either of us were of the mind set that in order to be a person of worth we had to have certain specialized qualities and yet we were lacking, we would both be in trouble. I can't sew; my wife can. She does not like to drive in traffic; it doesn't both me in the least. I burn water on the stove; she is an excellent cook. She is timid around the computer when tackling complex spreadsheets; I am fairly comfortable on the computer. The list could be multiplied for many pages but you get the idea. As you do your inventory of talents and abilities, don't be so short-sighted that you believe your differences cannot be as important to the success of your marriage as are the areas of commonality.

Before looking further into the value of differences, it would be well to note that if you have no areas of common interest, your relationship will be strained from the very beginning. Assuming that you have identified the common ground, how do you maximize the differences you possess?

Although I am interested in developing in all areas, realistically life is not long enough for me to become an expert in all areas. Therefore it is necessary to prioritize the areas I want to improve in. Then I can systematically work my way through until death interrupts the self- improvement process. Unless I take control of my time, I may well exit this life without having accomplished what I really want to, because I haven't taken the time to decide what I really want to do. Although the list changes periodically, there are still areas of improvement that I want to focus on. In the meantime, many of the areas that are still future on my list of things to master, my wife has already mastered.

Many young couples during the early days of marriage refuse to admit where they have talents. Either through false modesty or unwillingness to be totally honest with yourself, you may be downplaying areas of your expertise. How do you honestly, but without boasting, evaluate your strengths? Look first at the things you like to do. We generally like to do the things we are good at. A friend has a knack for fixing small engines. While I can change a spark plug or fill the engine with gas and maybe even change the oil, that is the extent of my talents. For years he downplayed his talent although everyone in the neighborhood brought their small engines to him for help in getting them running and keeping them in good shape. A couple of years ago he finally realized that he had a real talent. He has since gone into business repairing small engines and is making a very comfortable living.

It may require that you listen carefully to what other people are saying about you. If they do not have an ulterior motive for praising you (i.e. they need your help or think you can enhance their social, economic, or political position), they are apt to be honest and truthful. Even if you do not see the characteristic or trait in yourself, you should seriously consider what they say. As both of you begin to compile a list of strengths, be cautiously honest about those areas where you are not expert. People waste an incredible amount of time and money trying to do those things which an expert can do quickly, professionally, and usually incur less expense. One of the signs of true intelligence is to recognize your lack of expertise and know where to find someone who is an expert to do the work for you. The president of most of the huge corporations in the world are not experts in the products their corporations produce. They are just experts at surrounding themselves with people who do have those talents. They are paid enormous salaries because of their unique talents for organization and motivation and vision. Should we do any less in our marriage?

After having compiled the list of your strengths, note important areas where neither of you have much talent. One of you will need to develop the talent or at least know where to turn for help when the deficient area of expertise is needed. For example, if neither of you are good at handling money, you would be igniting the fuse on a huge marital explosion unless one or both of you get some training. If that doesn't work, you would need to employ the help of someone who has a talent in budgeting. Far too many marriages end in divorce over failure to recognize and eliminate the deficiency in financial planning. Usually a good friend or relative is more than willing to spend some time with you to teach you to budget and control your financial lives.

When we fail to recognize and appreciate that the best ideas have yet to be thought of, we run the risk of duplicating the mistake of a certain senator at the beginning of the twentieth century. He concluded that every possible invention had been patented and so closing the patent office would be in the best interest of the government. For those of us living during the final years of that same century, it is inconceivable that anyone would have seriously considered such a thought. It is nearly impossible to keep up with the information explosion. The prospects for the future are mind-boggling. We fully expect that the latest, greatest inventions of the

1990's will be laughed at as archaic within a very few short years.

Why do we then think that the best ideas about how to make a marriage work have been thought of? Are there those who propose that we close the marital patent office because everything has been tried that possibly could be envisioned in the mind of man? In just a few short years, we will take the ideas which seem so powerful and innovative today and laugh at them as dinosaurs of the past.

Although I am not an advocate of the extreme, radical movements which seem to take their generational toll every few years, I am not for maintaining status quo in our marital relationships. It seems that the young people starting in marriage today are more creative, more innovative, more visionary than their parents or grandparents of a generation earlier. For example, try getting your grandmother or grandfather to use your computer. Unless they are truly remarkable people, they will cower back in fear. Their lack of familiarity with the computer has probably generated false ideas about how they will destroy the computer if they hit the wrong key. You may reassure them until you are exhausted that they can't hurt the machine nor the programs, but usually to no avail. They have a mind set and they are not about to change.

We run a risk of doing the same thing in marriage. There are certain ways our parents do things and we are not about to entertain the idea of change. When questioned, we probably do not know why our parents do things the way they do. There isn't any compelling motivation to cause us to mimic their behavior. But we do anyway. We have had some major success in our marriage by daring to change some of those old ways of doing things which, upon closer inspection, really didn't have any solid rationale for doing them the way our families have done them for years. While it is probably true that our families look upon us as being different, it is also true that they seem to respect the progress we have made as a couple and a family.

I would recommend that you sit down as a couple and identify as many of those senseless habits as you can. Some of them are not bad, they are just there. Other habits really inhibit the progress of your marital relationship. Recently several of our young friends have terminated their marriages. When questioned about the causes, too frequently they say that the final, lethal blow was when the husband starting treating the new wife the same way his father treated his mother. If the perpetual "put down" is the environment you have grown up in, it is difficult to eliminate that from your behavior. Difference here is the key to not only marital happiness but also marital survival.

Don't be different just to be different. All change is not progress. It requires some serious adult thinking to find workable solutions to well-established family traditions. It is simple to identify the things you would like to change. It is far more challenging to find an acceptable alternative. When you are willing to investigate alternate ways of solving problems, you will discover that your differences are invaluable. If everyone used the same logic to arrive at possible solutions to problems, there would be no variety to the proposed solutions. The native differences between two distinct individuals let alone two very unique families, tends to result in a variety of possible solutions.

As you consider the different solutions proffered by each partner in the marriage, be very slow to make summary judgments and strike down a suggestion as "stupid" merely because it is different from what you have thought of or suggested. One of the "revelations" which caused me the most chagrin was to discover that many of the suggestions that our children had for solving problems were actually better than the ones I had suggested. After all, I was the one with the doctor's degree—they were still in elementary school. Nevertheless, when I matured and stopped looking at all differences of opinion as an attack on my ego, we started having a lot more fun as a family in solving problems. Occasionally the children will still let me try one of my ideas, so I'm not completely shelved because of my old age. With six children and a wife who are all very creative, there is seldom a lack of creative, different ideas for solving any problem we face.

Now we are at the end of our child-rearing experience and starting into the grand-parenting phase. Finally, instead of being offended when someone has a different idea, I have come to realize how blessed we are to have so many differences. Instead of trying to make everyone into a clone of mom or dad, we have stressed that they develop into their own person. Each has unique talents and interests. Each has ideas different from the rest. Some of the differences require more tolerance and patience by the other members of the family. But we will all agree (to the person!) that the differences have contributed to the overall beauty of the family.

One daughter summed it up this way, "When you look at a mountain scene the pine trees are beautiful. If that was all we ever saw mile after mile, it would soon get old and we would lose interest. When there are maples, quakies, oaks, etc. mixed in, it adds variety which increases (not decreases) the beauty of the scene." She was exactly on! If everyone dressed alike, it would make for boring people-watching no matter what the style and color of the clothing was. If everyone had the same sounding voice, the same color of hair, the same height and weight, the same everything—people would be pretty boring. Then it would be true "if you've seen one, you've seen them all!" Thankfully, that is not the case. God seems to relish individuality—look at the masses of humanity. No two of them are exactly alike. Even identical twins are different. Do we then propose to improve upon what God has done by making everyone exactly like everyone else in the marriage and family? That would be a fiasco.

So everything from the kinds of food we favor to the brands of soap we prefer adds to the diversity and beauty of the family. From the music we listen to all the way to the makes and models of cars we like, everything adds to the spice and flavor of life we enjoy. From the television shows we watch to the books we read, all enrich our world. From the hobbies we enjoy to the academic interests we pursue, all make for an interesting, challenging world. Be secure enough in yourself so that you don't misinterpret every difference as a challenge to your self worth—nothing could be further from the truth. The more comfortable we are with the diversity, the more enjoyable life becomes. The less threatened we are when someone has a "better idea" and the more open we are to discovering those un-patented marital inventions which will create a new level of enjoyment for an entire world in the next generation.

16

NON-COMPETE CLAUSE IN MARRIAGE

— ♥ —

It is tough to grow up in a world where there are limited spaces at the top. There is only one gold medal per athletic event, only one president of the company, only one President of the United States, only one super bowl championship team, etc. If we are not careful, we find ourselves transferring that same thinking to our marriages. Is there a "top dog" in marriage? Who should be the ultimate leader in the home? If the wife takes a subservient role to the husband, does that mean she is inferior or a second-rate citizen? If you buy into the dog-eat-dog philosophy of the world, your marriage is doomed to be a power struggle from day one unless one or both of you is a spineless fish. If you decide there is a more productive way, it could be the key to the success which separates you from the majority of marriages which end in such bitter divorces.

There isn't a number one in marriage. The two of you, according to the Bible (see Matthew 19:6) are no longer two but have become "one flesh." In other words, before you were married you were just half a person. Now you have added the other half and you "twain shall be one flesh." Another analogy that may help clarify this concept is a pair of scissors. If you disassemble the scissors you will have two parts that equal the same weight, the same bulk, the same attributes that the pair had while connected together. However, their functionality is entirely destroyed when they are separated. Try cutting a clean, straight line through a piece of paper with either half of the separated scissors. You will make a mess of the paper in a hurry. Combine the two halves as they were originally designed and you have an instrument that can perform a function which would be impossible for either half to accomplish by itself.

When a couple succumbs to the temptation to compete in marriage, they develop an adversarial relationship. Instead of doing all they can do to enhance their relationship, they selfishly guard any perceived advantage lest the other partner should take a position of superiority. Subtle little comments can weaken and undermine the relationship. Although said in apparently the purest of motives, the possible hidden meaning leaves doubt in the mind of the spouse. Not to be outclassed or caught flatfooted, the companion spouse often responds by making a comment which could still be innocent but perhaps has undertones of sarcasm which are not as well-veiled as the initial comment. Before long, unless recognized and checked early, the comments turn from masked digs and cuts to open, malicious, condescending remarks with no redeeming value.

When a marriage partner sees their spouse as an extension of himself or herself, it is easy to see how in the genuine complimenting of your spouse you only enhance your own status. After all, the person you chose to marry certainly casts a reflection on your ability to choose! The better my wife looks, the smarter it makes me look. The more I cut her down, the more I am parading before the ever-critical public my foolishness in deciding to marry her in the first place. The more honors and praise that come to the individuals in the marriage, the more status the entire institution of marriage receives. It would be foolish to say or do anything that would tear down the image your marriage has achieved.

So, assuming you agree that you should not compete in marriage, how do you accomplish such an elusive goal? Start by building each other up. If the comment you are about to make is not calculated to build, enhance, solidify, or move your marriage forward (as well as your mate), then don't make it. It would be impossible for you to read this book without knowing that I am adamantly opposed to ignoring problems and playing as if they didn't exist. That is lethal to any marriage. But to dwell on the negative, as though making your mate look bad in some distorted way makes you look better, is childish at best and relationship destroying at worst.

From the very wedding day (or long before), start looking at yourselves as a team. Eliminate saying "I" and "me" when referring to your marriage. Use "we" and "our" and the sense of team will increase dramatically. Once we began to master talking in the plural, our friends would ask: "We? Are you pregnant?" when I would be making a comment without my wife being present. I would respond in the negative about me being pregnant but explain that the decisions we made as husband and wife affected us both and so the decision was not mine or hers but "ours." Before long we noticed that they too were talking in the plural. Occasionally I would taunt them a little with their challenge: "We? Are you pregnant?" We would laugh and move on to the next topic of conversation. Maybe it is too idealistic or simplistic to draw a one-on-one association, but none of the fifteen couples who were in our group while we were growing up have divorced.

It didn't take very long after the honeymoon to realize that my new bride was my greatest fan. She was always telling her friends how thoughtful I was, how neat I was, how generous I was, etc. I didn't want to make a liar of her so I tried a little harder to be thoughtful, generous and neat. In turn I found it natural to tell others how creative, how loving, how self-sacrificing, how truly beautiful etc. my wife was. She became in my eyes everything I said she was. If that is true in marriage, (i.e. that your mate becomes exactly what you say they are!), what kind of mate will you have? If you are not satisfied with what you've got, try building each other up rather than airing faults before family, friends, and the world.

When you begin to develop the team spirit, you soon realize that "two heads really are better than one." Often I become so busy in the day-to-day rush of keeping up that I fail to do the little thoughtful things that cements friendships. Often a person will stop me on the street and thank me for some kind gesture, some thoughtful card, a bouquet of flowers, a plate of cookies, etc. that we sent them in a time of need. At first I tried to determine what they were talking about by asking them directly. I soon learned that it was more productive and image enhancing to ask my wife what she had done. I don't know why I'm not as thoughtful as my wife, but I'm not, even though I've been working on it for years. All I know is that the little things she does makes us look like wonderfully considerate people. While it is true that I finance the flowers, cards, etc. it is more accurate to say that few, if any, of the truly thoughtful things of life would be accomplished if my wife left it up to me. Seems like a good team effort—I provide the funds, she provides the thoughtful service. No competition, just mutual cooperation. No "Number 1," just one special team. I'm really glad we're on the same team.

The world can be a mean place. At times I go home after a trying day and want to climb into a cocoon and not come out again. It is a thoughtful team member who meets me at the door and in spite of the challenges of her day, puts me together before sharing her burdens with me. I know I should be the strong one to help her unburden the challenges associated with child rearing, but it seems like she is usually a step or two ahead of me in lifting my burden before easing her own. We have found that one form of friendly competition is healthy in our marriage. We try to see who can be the first to inquire how the other's day has gone. Sometimes I'll ask and she will respond by asking how my day has gone. If I'm not careful, I'll catch myself unloading on her all the challenges of the day, at which time she smiles and I know that she has bested me. On other occasions, I catch the sly fox and respond by saying, "Don't try to reverse the question. Tell me first how your day has been!" Then she knows I caught her in the act of trying to gain advantage over me by her very caring gesture. We sometimes laugh a lot as we jockey for the advantage position. Even the laughter seems to ease part of the burden of the day.

Another place where living in a basically negative world can be hurtful is the things people say that are not true or that are not kind. Gossip is a poison which is hard to purge from your system. People seem to enjoy passing on a tidbit of gossip even if they know or suspect that it is untrue or only partially true. Women, often being the more sensitive, are more likely to take the gossip more seriously than men. Here the husband (or wife) can be a great healer as you put the gossip into proper perspective. When we deal with falsehoods in the highly emotional state of anger or fear, we often say or do things which only compounds the problem. When the loving, sensitive mate can help put things into proper perspective, overreacting is kept to a minimum or eliminated altogether. Some of our most humorous and stress-relieving experiences have been the sessions of uncontrolled laughter as we realized how ridiculous the gossip was and how incredible the accusation sounded even to us.

If we have not been wise enough to hold our peace until the emotion has calmed, we have often spent far too much time trying to repair the damage our rash actions have caused. For the benefit of your marriage, be a true team and watch out for each other lest one or both of you get blind-sided. If you find that you are both angry together, agree to disengage from the situation until you are both more calm, collected, and in control. If you have difficulty seeing the wisdom in what I am saying, try reacting in anger to some malicious gossip and watch the fallout. Then try reacting as I have suggested and the difference will convince you that I have taught a correct principle.

Another serious area where the non-compete clause is essential is in rearing children. If either or both of you jockey for a favored position with the children, you will all be losers—you, your spouse, and the children. There is a definite role for the father and a distinct role for the mother. The love of a child need not be limited to one at the exclusion of the other. Love is not a commodity of limited quantity. There may be times during the growing years when a child seeks the mother's advice more than the father's. Don't be too hasty in feeling like the child favors the mother. In a short time the tables may turn and the child seeks the advice of the father before going to the mother. If both mother and father are on the same team, there isn't a score card kept to determine which one's counsel is sought more often. If the two of you are truly one, then the most important thing is that the child feels comfortable enough to get advice from either of you.

In a day when most women work outside the home, it is easy to fall into the trap where you compete in earning power. Who has the largest take-home income? If you are really a single team, the amount of the earned income is a nonissue. However much each makes only enriches the team. If you have successfully completed your talents and resources inventory, you may discover that the wife has a more marketable talent than the husband at this point in time. It would be foolish not to maximize her earning opportunities. Caution needs to be taken, however, because immediate short-term gain may be overshadowed by long term potential earning power. For example, a wife may have a super job as a senior secretary in a law firm—big bucks right now. However, her top end earning potential is dwarfed by the potential long-term income of the husband when he finishes law school or medical school. Be wise enough to evaluate your financial moves with the long-range future in mind rather than focusing exclusively on the immediate.

Only the two of you can prioritize your long-range goals. Wonderful contributions have been made in law, medicine, politics, etc. by women whose husbands have agreed to allow them to pursue their careers at the expense of the husband taking second seat in his career. Moving to Washington D.C. while a wife serves in congress may postpone or even prevent the husband from achieving his long term goals in his chosen profession. Usually it is not so dramatic. Both of you can accomplish your goals with some compromise and a lot of understanding and hard work. If pursuing one's goals precluded the other from accomplishing his or her goals, then you must make an informed decision built on information and agreement. It is a given that neither or both of you can be everything to everybody. Life seems to be so designed that difficult choices must be made which automatically close the doors on other possible dreams.

Whatever your circumstances may be, you can only be winners if you stay on the same team. With a world apparently bent on tearing you apart, you need all the resolve you can muster to stick to each other through the tough times as well as the good times. A lonely superstar at the top of the social or political ladder is bound to experience more loneliness and unhappiness than those married people who are involved in each other's worlds to the extent that they couldn't conceive of living without each other.

How do you determine whose career comes first? That isn't always easy to do. If you have the maturity, try to establish what you want your roles to be when the children are married and moved away and the grandchildren come back to visit. Although that time seems far away when you are first married, it arrives with surprising rapidity as the years silently pass almost unnoticed. We decided early on that the role of Grandma was the most important role in both our lives excluding our parents. Therefore my wife and I chose to have her emphasis placed in the homemaking role rather than establishing a career outside the home. Occasionally people will ask: "Does your wife work?" My answer, which reflects our mutually agreed upon response, is always: "Yes, much harder than I do—but not outside the home." Anyone who has ever tried to keep a household running smoothly with half a dozen little kids knows exactly what we are talking about. Compared to the multifaceted demands placed on my wife, my job of teaching and counseling is a piece of cake.

Does my wife feel like a second-rate citizen because she chose to be a full-time mom? I guess you would have to ask her, but if you can believe her response, I can tell you she looks at her work in rearing the next generation as more important than my job of earning a living. Has she felt the pressure to "get a degree," "establish a career," "help earn a living," etc. which so many women today say they feel? Yes, definitely. But when we talked about the division of labor in our family before we were married, we agreed that I would earn the money and she would protect our greatest assets— our children. Does she regret the choice we made while we were so young and inexperienced? She adamantly insists that she does not. Now with the children almost raised, she can, if she chooses, go back to school and finish her degree. She may go back, she may not. She learned along the way that having a college degree does not make you any more of a person than not having one. She learned one of the great lessons of life—being schooled and being educated are only remotely associated. Many unschooled people are very highly educated people. Some of the "dumbest" people I know are those with the most degrees or letters behind their names.

Because we both recognized the importance of having her home with the children during their formative years, we decided that I would work two jobs rather than her working outside the home. Maybe that decision isn't right for you two, or maybe it isn't even a possibility, but it has paid great dividends for us. I have, parenthetically, worked two jobs most of our married life. We feel we made the right decision. Does she feel like she is beholding to me for any money she gets to spend? Absolutely not. In fact, I am the one who often has been reluctant to take from the family piggy bank to spend for myself. Remember, we view ourselves as a team and not as two competing individuals.

The reason I am sharing this very intimate and personal insight into our marriage is not to gloat or suggest that what we decided is best for everyone. The real reason is to show you how the world around you subtly puts pressure on you to conform to its unwritten code of expectations. Professional women have at times made condescending remarks about my wife not working outside the home or finishing her college education before having children. If she had been willing to allow their thoughtless comments to wound her, she would have been dead long ago. It took almost a quarter of a century of deflecting their verbal jabs but now she seldom, if ever, hears those criticisms. You see, none of our six children has ever been arrested, been busted for DUI, stolen anything from a store, taken drugs, failed out of school, joined a gang, become involved in premarital sex, or any of the other delinquent things plaguing today's youth.

Is that kind of a track record due to the fact that their dad has a doctor's degree and works with young people every day? That could have something to do with it, but the real reason is that their mother was there at the door when they left for school (I was not!), and when they returned home (I was not!). In fact I was absent from the home a great deal when the kids really needed parental guidance. Thankfully, their self-sacrificing mother was there and provided the anchor necessary to keep them from being tossed out of control on the turbulent seas of shifting values. No, the credit does not belong to me. It belongs to my wife.

So many of those critical, professional women have sought counsel from my wife on how to cope with the problems their children are encountering. We don't gloat or point the finger of blame—that is totally nonproductive. She does counsel from her huge reservoir of practical experience to help them reclaim children who (at least momentarily) have abandoned many of their family values in exchange for the latest fad or craze.

Can you, even this early in your lives, envision what life will be like when you both are confined to wheelchairs on the front porch? Because we were and are a team, and refuse to compete with each other, we have successfully avoided (to this point!) many of the frustrations so common to those who didn't take the time to think further down the line. You are in a unique position. You are about to be married or have just recently married. Now is the time to establish a team mentality and then stick to your decisions. If our experience is remotely typical, you will never regret your decision to resist every temptation to become competitors.

17

NOT ALLOWING CHILDREN TO COME BETWEEN YOU

— ♥ —

About the time you figure you have mastered the art of getting along as husband and wife, you discover that you are going to have a baby. It is almost comical how something no larger than a pencil lead and not even visibly present can have such a profound effect on your relationship. Nothing is the same after the doctor confirms that you are pregnant.

If the pregnancy was planned and expected, then joy and excitement are the natural results. If pregnancy was a surprise, it may take some getting used to before the fear, worry, and mental anguish give way to joy and excitement. Usually, a young couple (even if the pregnancy was not planned) become elated as the birth draws near.

There is so much to do, so much to buy, so many preparations to make. If you think your life was complicated before, just wait until the baby arrives! In those intervening months between the conception and the birth, the sheer number of details that you must address as a couple has a welding influence on your marriage. Even if the husband is not excited about the prospects of increasing the size of the family, it is helpful to get him involved as much as possible in the planning, purchasing, and making ready for the baby. Everything you do together increases the anticipation of the blessed event.

When the baby is actually born, you have the first tangible result of your marriage. That baby is literally a combination of its father and mother. During those first few weeks, it is not uncommon for both the husband and wife to hover over the baby constantly. Then the newness of the baby's presence wears off and couples must settle down to the routine of life. Usually the husband must go back to work, the wife's attention, strength, emotional energy, etc. are absorbed to the point of depletion by that one mini-human being. It is usually the mother who must bear the majority of the responsibility for meeting the infant's needs. Right or wrong, the husband is not mechanically (physically!) equipped to feed the baby if it is to be breast fed. How can one so small require so much care?

If the baby happens to get its schedule mixed up, he or she may be up most of the night and sleep most of the day. That only adds to the mounting frustration. It almost seems like your lives are not your own any more. That could be because that's a true analysis. For the next number of years both of you will (hopefully without regret or disdain) surrender your own personal wants and desires for the good of the children. Occasionally couples look longingly back to the "old days" when life was so simple. Some even wish they could return but since that isn't a possibility, it does little or no good to dwell on what will never be—at least for a number of years.

The vast majority of parents gladly accept the inconvenience of disrupted schedules, unusual demands, and major modifications in the routine of life in order to enjoy the overwhelming joy of having a new baby in the home. As the child grows it is easy to stay interested. He or she is learning so many things so quickly that there is always something new to "ooh and ah" about. The first step, the first word, the first smile, the first everything is so novel that it commands attention.

If you decide to add another child, the entire process is repeated, but this time there are even more demands because the first child didn't just disappear. When there is only one child, the parents outnumber him or her two to one. When the second arrives it is still a one-on-one situation. Although that isn't exactly true because little children have so much more energy than the parents that they never seem to run down. After two children the parents are definitely outnumbered.

Now comes the potential problems. Without constant attention, the baby will die. Therefore you are left without choice that you must meet their needs. As they grow the needs are compounded by wants. The needs and wants are further compounded by demands the refusal of which may result in temper tantrums.

The serious challenge for this book is to raise the warning flag that with all the demands of earning a living and raising children, it is almost too easy to let the children come between you as husband and wife. When the wife hovers over the children at the expense of paying attention to the husband, there is a potentially fatal flaw in the marital relationship. At that point the husband may decide to look elsewhere for the affection which the wife is not as willing to share because of sheer physical and emotional fatigue. It requires understanding and cooperation to avoid making those kinds of mistakes.

How do you keep the demands of children from coming between you? Just like every other problem you have or will face, it requires that the two of you evaluate the potential problem, and find a creative solution before it becomes a monster requiring major effort to defeat. When we discovered the problems starting to arise as I was working full-time, holding down a part-time job, working on a master's degree, and being very active in church and civic affairs and my wife being totally absorbed in two little girls, homemaking, church and civic affairs, we decided not to allow the rush of life to separate us. Because money was a premium in those early days (i.e. we didn't have a lot of discretionary funds beyond those committed to the essentials), we traded baby-sitting with other young couples who were in our same situation. We would take their children for a couple of hours while they went for a walk, or took in a movie, or had a picnic in the park, or went to the free museum, etc. In turn they would watch our little girls while we escaped for a few hours to regain our sanity and re-cement our relationship. It didn't require much. Just a date a week seemed to do wonders for both of us. Some of our dearest and lifelong friends are those couples with whom we traded free babysitting.

The anticipation of our time together gave us both something to look forward to. We seldom invited others to join our dates in those early years. Time alone without the kids was difficult to arrange and we really needed the time without the added pressure of entertaining friends. In later years we spent more time with friends and even took their kids and ours on the picnics. But by that time the kids were old enough to tend themselves so it wasn't an added burden on us.

As the children mature, that too is a mixed blessing. They are able to take care of most of their own needs—that is good. They have also learned to talk and reason a little—that is good and bad. Good because you can give them directives and they understand what you are telling them. Bad when they learn how to pit mom against dad in their attempts to get what they want. It is amazing to me how soon young children learn to manipulate parents. It is almost unfair.

If you know you have been blessed with one of those manipulators as a child, it is wise to sit down and take control of the situation. We have one so I am speaking from personal experience. Whenever this son can't get what he wants from his mother, he comes to me. It just took a couple of times to realize he was playing us against each other. His childish logic went like this: "Dad, mom said it was all right if I went to play with my friend if it was all right with you." It took a little communication between my wife and I to discover that he had just used the inverse rationale on her: "Mom, dad said it was all right if I went to play with my friend if it was all right with you." Not wanting to countermand each other, we let him go play where a direct question to either of us would have resulted in a negative answer because it was nearing dinner time.

Solving the problem was easy. We agreed (my wife and I) that if our son ever phrased the inquiry like that we would either say: "Let's go talk to mom together," at which time he would immediately know he was caught. Or I would say: "If I check with your mother and find you are playing us against each other, you will be grounded for the next week from playing with your friends. Think it over and see if mom really told you it was OK." Using that logic, he could see that it wasn't worth chancing a week-long grounding for one unwarranted hour of play with a friend. He wasn't (and isn't) a bad kid. He just had watched his friends play their parents against each other and win.

Another critical time comes when children start to have problems getting along with their friends. Sometimes they want parents to jump in and solve the problems by disciplining their friends. Some unwise parents become part of the childish squabbles and the problems escalate in a hurry. The problem is when the mother or the father spends an inordinate amount of time listening to and trying to help the children solve their problems at the expense of taking time for their spouse. While it is commendable to give training, counsel, and advice to your children to help them learn the complex and difficult social skills, it is not appropriate to spend that time at the expense of spending necessary time with your mate.

Whenever the children take a position preeminent to the spouse, you are asking for trouble. In a very few short years the children will develop their own set of friends, then they are off to college, then they are married, and you two are left alone. If you have hovered over the children at the expense of the marital relationship, you are left with an empty shell of a relationship after the children have left home. It requires a constant effort to avoid such a tragic situation. It is disheartening to read of so many couples who have been married for thirty, forty, and even fifty years who are now divorcing. You can bet they are not divorcing because they are so much in love and have so many things in common.

If couples take the time to keep the love alive by constantly fanning the flames of love, if they stay a vital part of each other's world by constantly doing things together, then when the children leave home, they are given a second (extended) honeymoon that can and will last for years. You may need to think this principle through and make sure it fits for you. Even if some of the demands of the children are not met, they seem to survive. We have found that it is virtually impossible to meet all of the demands of all six of our children. Your fragile marriage will not last if neglected until the endless multitude of demands of the children are met.

Another crisis comes later in life when your children marry and then go through the normal adjustments that you and your spouse are going through or will shortly go through. Often they react as though they were the very first couple on earth to be challenged with the problems they are facing. Your wise counsel can help them understand that what they are experiencing is normal. However, when serious marital conflict develops between your child and their spouse, it is a temptation to "take sides." By doing so you are exposing your marriage to some serious stress. This is especially true if one of you agrees with your child and one of your agrees with their spouse. I have seen marriages destroyed not because of the problems within the marriage itself but the problems within the marriages of their children.

How can you avoid this pitfall? Who jumped in and solved all of your problems for you? The answer is no one! That is also the same person who should help your children solve their problems. The growth you will experience as a young married couple as you struggle to overcome the challenges of life will cement your marriage. Why would you deny your children the same bonding experience? There is nothing wrong with meeting problems and being forced to creatively overcome them. You may choose to give them some mutual advice. I would strongly recommend that you refuse to become embroiled in their conflicts.

If your children refuse to take your advice or to follow your example, then they must learn the hard way. That is the way life is set up. Remember, there are lessons of life to learn. You may learn them by being taught or you can learn them by sad experience— but learn them you will. No child's problems is important enough to sabotage your marriage. All that would accomplish is the destruction of two marriages—yours and theirs.

A final problem to consider in not allowing children to come between you is the tendency to underestimate your child's ability to cope without your help. Some mothers and fathers refuse to cut the strings and let their children evolve into responsible adults themselves. An elderly friend of mind (now deceased) told me that his mother-in-law divorced her husband so she could move in with her daughter and her husband. The mother-in-law was so sure that the daughter couldn't cope without her constant supervision, that she sacrificed her own marriage. "Grandma," as they called her, lived with them until she died just a few years before I became acquainted with my friend. I was dumbfounded. I couldn't believe 1) she would do such a thing, and 2) that they would permit it. I'm afraid my wife would have had to make a choice from the very beginning—either me or her mother. Thankfully that kind of occurrence is rare.

However, it is not rare for parents to feel obliged to give constant input into the marriage of their children. It would be well if the two of you seriously considered how you would react if both your parents continually interfered in your marriage. Just contemplating your reaction, you will readily recognize the inadvisability of that kind of an arrangement. Then, if you wouldn't appreciate it (or if it is already a reality—you don't appreciate it!), then avoid perpetuating the problem into the next generation.

As much as any other problem I deal with in marriage counseling is the friction caused by well-meaning but misdirected parents interfering in the marital affairs of their children. So whether the divisive influence comes from your parents or from your children, it should be an immediate red flag. Take immediate action (or better—preventative action) now to eliminate the problem. You may need to be creative and firm in solving the problem.

There is a simple analogy which may help cement the concepts discussed in this chapter. If you consider your marriage as the "mothership" in a space voyage and the children are little space-ships who venture out on exploratory missions, then you can see the inadvisability of destroying the mothership in order to travel with the individual spaceships. In fact your goal is to train each little spaceship to become a mothership for the next generation of space travelers. Don't allow your mothership (i.e. your parents' marriages) to destroy your right to develop into a mothership of your own. Don't you prevent your little spaceships from developing into motherships for the next generation.

The two of you form the most important relationship on earth—husband and wife. Children come and children go. Parents live and parents die. But the two of you form a unit that can resemble a bit of heaven on earth if you never allow anyone or anything to come between you—including your own children.

18

PUTTING PRIORITIES ON TIME AND RESOURCES

— ♥ —

There are many people in the world who seem to have the attitude that activity is progress. As long as something is going on, it must be a sign that things are progressing well. Unfortunately, the same is true in marriage. Just because everyone is busy and a lot of activity is taking place, it is dangerous to conclude that the marriage is healthy. It requires some skill and patience to cut through the maze of activity and correctly diagnose the state of health of the marriage. How can you do it? It isn't that difficult but it requires that you set a standard against which you can measure your marriage.

If you start out on a trip with a specific destination five hundred miles away, it requires more than just ten hours of driving at fifty miles per hour. You also must be traveling in the most direct route towards your destination to arrive there in ten hours. Detours, direct routes in the wrong direction, or circular traveling never helps you achieve your goal or destination. What do you want your marriage to be like fifty years from now? If you can carefully answer that question, you can determine your progress along the way. Perhaps you have grandparents who have an ideal marriage and you want to imitate them. More likely, there isn't a single couple who has everything exactly the way the two of you want. The ideal couple doesn't have to be real. They can be fictitious or a composite couple. But, as with the trip, if you have no specific destination, how will you know if you have arrived?

You will soon discover in marriage, as in life, that choices have to be made. Often those choices are not between good and bad, right and wrong, correct and incorrect. More often they are between several good things but of different priorities. For example, if you are planning to have a dinner date with your husband or wife and someone from the local Lion's club (of which you are a member) calls and needs your help at a conflicting time, which one do you do? If your priorities are well-established, the decision will not be difficult. If you are crisis oriented then whichever demand screams the loudest gets the time and attention.

Is there a right and wrong list of priorities? A better question might be: "can we agree on the list of priorities for our marriage?" I have seen a variety of hierarchical lists. Some are simple and contain few items. Others are elaborate and have multiple items. Rather than just a "right or wrong" list, it is important that you have one that both of you agree upon. From the variety of lists I have seen over the years, let me suggest the one that seems to bear the most fruit when tried in the crucible of marriage.

First on the list is your spouse. If he or she is not number one, you run the risk of having a saddle with no horse. In other words, unless your spouse has top priority, you may have everything else in the world and be a miserable, single person. Often when people call for my professional services, I check the calendar and, noting a planned activity with my wife, I say: "I'm sorry, I have a prior commitment." Never once has the person asked "what is it?" or "can't you postpone it so you can accommodate my request?" If the request is something that is important, I may talk over with my wife the possibility of rescheduling our planned activity. If she is reluctant or the planned activity doesn't permit rescheduling, we simply do what we had planned and refuse to feel guilty for not responding to the other request. After all, why should we feel guilty when we have put top priority things in first place?

We borrowed our second priority from an older couple who seemed to have the ideal family. Since adopting it ourselves, I have noticed that a majority of really successful couples seem to have the same priority: "children come next on the priority list just under the spouse." In the last chapter we discussed the potential pitfall of putting children before your spouse. That would be a wrong move to make. If the children are taught from the time they are able to understand that the most important relationship in the home is between mom and dad, they will begin to see that the stability of their world depends on their cooperating while mom and dad do whatever is necessary to make sure their marriage is solid. If mom and dad's marriage breaks up, it destroys the children's world as well.

When more than one child is involved, it requires fairness and constant vigilance to insure that one child is not favored over the others. If children cooperate in a marriage, your life is infinitely easier. If they do not cooperate, they have the power to make your life a living nightmare. Putting them next on the priority scale to your spouse all but insures that they will sense how valuable they are to the family. When they sense "ownership" in the family, they have a vested interest in making the family successful rather than sabotaging it. You may wonder why I didn't list your career as the second priority above the children. It may surprise you to find where so many successful couples actually rank their professional careers—read on.

The third priority is rather difficult to put into words without being misunderstood. I have seen men and women so absorbed in their mates and children that they almost lose their own identity. Particularly young mothers who happen to have babies close together (a choice often agreed upon by the couples so the children will grow up best friends and playmates). Unless some attention is given to the continued development of her own talents and interests, she can easily find herself a professional housecleaner, cook, diaper changer, and communicator in monosyllables. Unless detected and corrected, she soon sees herself in an endless role of meeting everyone else's needs with no prospects of having her needs met in the immediate future. Discouragement and despondency are often the result. In a fit of frustrated fatigue, too many otherwise faithful wives seek romantic attention outside the home. That impulsive fling can cost them their husband and children and the genuinely happy home they had planned.

With very little effort and a little planning, the need to look elsewhere can be eliminated. As you plan together how you are going to reach your destination of continued growth for each of you, you will likely see the importance of planning time for the spouse to be away from the children and pursue interests of his or her own. An art class offered through the community, a skiing class at the local resort, a dance class for the two of you together, a membership in the local health club—the list multiplies as you identify those talents and interests that you both want to pursue either individually or together. Without planning, you can rest assured that the press of normal living will expand to fill your entire day. Nothing of value just happens. You must plan to make time for your personal development.

You have probably noticed people who seem to have enough time to do everything. They never seemed to be in a hurry or overly stressed. If you look closely you will notice that they have the same number of hours in their day as you have. They have just taken control of their lives by putting higher priority items nearer the top of their list. They will readily admit that there are many things they would like to do but just do not have the time to do them. In other words, those items are lower on their priority list than the activities in which you see them participating.

If you ignore personal development, you may succeed in raising your family, providing a living, even having a good time doing service for others, but when the children leave the nest and your health begins to become a factor you must consider before engaging in activities, you may discover, too late, that you should have been more diligent in keeping your priority list straight.

The fourth priority for many people deals with their spiritual lives. How involved do you care to be in your church? By mutual agreement the decision to participate regularly in church services and activities puts an "other world or next world" perspective in your marriage. If you focus too much on the "now" and never consider the long range future, you may find that when you arrive in the distant future (which happens one day at a time!), you may sadly discover that you have excluded a priority item that millions of others have found to be rewarding and soulsatisfying. Consider carefully before ignoring your spiritual future.

You may actually be surprised that I have placed church activity fourth on the list. I am aware that the Ten Commandments commands us to put God first in our lives. I certainly am not disputing the preeminent place which God should occupy in each individual's life. However, you may find that your faith in and devotion to God is separate from your activity in church services. While it is true that worshiping together with family and friends makes it easier to focus your attention on God, you will also find that your church may sponsor more activities than you can possibly keep up with in light of the other three higher priorities on your list.

Perhaps more important than the quantity of church-related activities you participate in would be the quality of devotion and service you render. You may choose to jockey the position of this item on your list. Whatever you decide, I urge you to take a hard, long-range look into the future before discarding it from your list altogether.

The fifth priority on my list (and the lists of many other stable families) is my profession or career or job. You may think that employers demand that your number one priority is working for them.

If that were the case with my employer, he would have one less (or at least a different!) employee. Long after the retirement date comes and passes, I hope to be a happily married man with a multitude of grandchildren and great-grandchildren around us. If they have taken second seat all of my working life—which is the majority of my life— then when I am ready to make them top priority, they are not interested. If you wait to establish the order of importance the children and grandchildren have in your life, they will not wait for you to decide. They will establish their priority lists and you needn't be surprised if you are way down near the bottom of their lists.

In putting work number five, I am certainly not suggesting that you take a casual, disinterested approach towards your profession. I honestly believe that you ought to be the very best you can possibly be in whatever profession or career you choose. Give an honest day's work for an honest day's pay. Make yourself so valuable to the company that they couldn't possibly do without you. Position yourself so you are the first one considered for promotion or a raise. None of those things are incompatible with your priority list.

If the work demands become so interruptive that your wife and children are suffering, talk with your boss. If he or she is so unsympathetic and unyielding that they will not make changes to accommodate your needs—then you plan on making a change to eliminate the conflict. If you are seen as valuable, even irreplaceable, you might be pleasantly surprised how company rules can be modified to keep you happy.

With our society as mobile as it is, you can almost plan on changing jobs half a dozen times during the forty or more years you are in the work force. Don't ever get to the point that you feel the job you are doing is the only one you can do. If you have your head screwed on straight, you will soon discover that you are one of a rare breed. People with principles, plans, and priorities are not easy to come by. You are being naive if you fail to see your value to any company you care to work for.

141

The final caution I will mention in this area is when you decide to go into business for yourself. Having done that, I am painfully aware that the forty-hour work week was not designed for entrepreneurs. Working for yourself, while rewarding and very satisfying, is also a very demanding job. You need to plan on and agree to many long hours before your business is well enough established to allow you the free time you generally associate with owning your own business. The real advantage to many family-owned businesses is that you can involve the entire family in the business. That sort of kills two birds with one stone—you build the business at the same time you spend more time with your spouse and children.

Before deciding that a family business is the direction you want to go, talk to several families who are currently (or have in the past) engaged in family businesses. Get them to share the pros and cons and then carefully consider whether you are prepared to pay the price. If you decide to do it, make it a family (at least a couple, if you have no children) decision.

The sixth and final item on the priority list for us and for many other successful families is the obligation you sense to your community, civic, and even political arena. If we shift the responsibility to create our neighborhood, city, state, etc. to others, then we need to be prepared to accept whatever kind of a world they create for us. If we don't like what we see happening around us, we need to get involved and work through the system to change things. All of that requires time and energy.

If you consider the result of totally ignoring your civic responsibility, you might come to the conclusion that unless everyone is controlling their families, you might not have a safe place where you can enjoy your family. Assess your talents and interests. It may be that you can coach a little league team or volunteer for community service including your family. By doing those things, you can again fulfill two of your commitments at the same time—your family and the community. If the community comes before your family or spouse, you may find that you are the most well thought-of citizen in the community but have no home life to enjoy as you mature or have spare time.

You can readily see the problem with trying juggle all six items simultaneously. That is why I've stopped at six! If you enlarge your list much beyond what I have mentioned, a growing sense of hopelessness may begin to engulf you. Even though you will never have enough time, energy, or resources to do everything you want to do, your frustration level will be greatly decreased if you keep your priorities straight.

I have noticed that the more energy you expend worrying about what you are not doing and feeling guilty for not being able to meet everyone's demands, the less effective you are in doing what you really want to do. Refuse to accept the guilt trips which are frequently laid upon you by those who have not taken the time to make their priority lists and therefore are more subject to the screaming demands of others whose lists are equally jumbled.

Being in control of your own time and resources gives a feeling of serenity and power. Enjoy being in control by establishing your priority list and refusing to let others control you.

19

AVOIDING THE WANDERING EYE (I) SYNDROME

— ♥ —

At first glance you might say: "I thought we have already discussed this issue in the chapter on "Being True to Each Other." That is correct. Therefore this chapter will deal with other potentially fatal practices which can threaten your marriage if ignored.

There are two aspects of this topic to be discussed separately: 1) focusing too much attention on personal wants and desires at the expense of your spouse— I call that having "I" problems; and 2) areas to be cautious about.

There is a cliche that has gained some prominence in the capitalistic society in which we live. It has a cutesy ring but certainly does not contribute to the solidity of your marriage: "If I don't watch out for number one, nobody else will." The meaning is clear—nobody watches out for your interests like you do. In marriage there is another person who gives as much or more attention to your interests than you do—your spouse. When a person becomes so absorbed in their own affairs, they are difficult to be around. Unless they see the direct benefit to themselves of an activity or project, they refuse to participate. If they are not particularly interested in a game or a play, they ignore the impact their attitude has on others and seek for some activity that meets their selfish fancy. It doesn't take too long until everyone else finds excuses to exclude them from the party list.

Our entire society, as well as the entirety of life to the point of marriage, fosters this kind of self-centeredness. We learned as infants that if our immediate needs were not being met, all we had to do was cry a little louder. Other people (usually our parents) dropped whatever they were doing and rushed to our aid. After a few years we realized that more of our own needs were to be met by ourselves and that others were not as willing to drop everything and rush to our assistance. Most of us successfully made the transition to performing our own tasks. An alarming number refused to make the change. Instead they started throwing temper tantrums. At the most embarrassing of all times, they would scream and cry; some would even pound their own heads on the floor in order to create such an embarrassing scene that the parents would give in to their demands rather than suffer the social mortification associated with the uncontrolled behavior. Probably the best thing would have been to walk off and leave them there to perform their tantrum to a very unsympathetic audience.

During the teen years many young people revert to their childish egocentrism. With little or no consideration for the impact their decisions have on other people, they go and come as they please. They label any attempts at parental control as abusive, domineering, excessive, and illegal. They are starting to develop into adults physically but an unnerving number are still very childish mentally. For the majority the body and mind begin to reunite before the last few teenage years. For a disquieting number, they refuse to grow up and resist assuming adult responsibility.

It is the latter group who pose an awful burden in marriage. They are so self-centered that they fail to consider that others have needs and rights as well as they. Not only does what they want have to take precedent over the wishes of others, but it must be done in the window of time they selfishly designate. Everything from sex on demand to impulse buying when funds are not available stand as stark examples of their lack of consideration. One frustrated young wife complained: "Why does my husband always wait until we are walking out the door, almost late for an appointment before he demands sex?" Is it a matter of control or just demanding his way and at his designated time?

When unchecked, "I" problems can increase the tension and pressure in a new marriage to the point of breaking. If you discover that either you or your mate has the problem to some degree, take time to establish controls to overcome the problem. It doesn't necessarily mean that you can never have your needs met. Perhaps realizing that others are watching out for your interests will ease the fear of going through life without any hopes of having your needs met. If our experience has been typical, the more you focus your attention on meeting the needs of your spouse and children, they more they reciprocate by trying to meet your needs. For some reason it is always more fun to mow the neighbor's lawn than my own. In other words, the tasks we do may be the same ones we would do to meet our own needs, but it is much more rewarding to do those same things for others and allow them the joy of doing some of your tasks for you.

There is no status quo in marriage or life. Either we are progressing towards our goals or retrogressing from them. You will soon discover that your marriage is equally dynamic. Either you are progressing towards an ideal marriage or you are becoming increasingly frustrated as your marriage slowly disintegrates. The reassuring thing is that you two have the power to decide which way your marriage will go. No marriage is destined from the beginning to end in divorce. Failure to recognize flaws or unwillingness to correct undesirable behaviors contribute to the demise of a beautiful relationship.

What areas pose problems that you would do well to attend to? I will mention only a few, but from the list you will be able to make your own list to meet your particular situation. Because sexual unfaithfulness is so prevalent (at least the media portrays it as the latest social epidemic to flood the country), it would be well to reiterate the caution. When the newness of sex has worn off after the honeymoon, take affirmative action to stay interested sexually in each other. As in so many other areas of life, talking openly and freely about your feelings, your likes and dislikes can have a very positive effect. Realizing, as mentioned earlier, that standing alone the glue of sexual attraction is not sufficiently strong to keep your marriage together forever, admit to each other that there may be cycles in your physical relationship that are normal and expected. Then when one or both of you are experiencing a lull in sexual interest, don't panic. Merely focus your attention in some other area and before long you'll both experience a pleasant rebound in sexual interest.

One major error that so many couples seem to commit is to think that they must find sexual fulfillment outside marriage when one of these lulls occur. The highway of marital bliss is literally littered with the broken remains of countless marriages where husbands and wives thought they could find happiness and fulfillment outside the marriage bonds. There is one thing for sure—if you disregard the counsel, you will be able to bear a personal testimony that the principle we are discussing is true. Save yourself the heartache and be faithful even when the fire is not burning so brightly.

Another area is uncontrolled spending or impulse buying. Too many times to mention I have been in counseling sessions with young couples who were being crushed with unmanageable debt (a topic we will address in detail later in the book). With minor variations the story is always the same. Either the husband or wife says: "I saw this thing and just had to have it. I never stopped to think about whether we could afford it or not." The "thing" can be anything from a jet ski to a dress to a car to a vacation, etc. The characteristic element is "I" saw and "I" wanted.

How do you curb such uncontrolled purchases? It really isn't that difficult. Just agree that you will discuss any purchase over a certain amount with each other before committing your family finances to that purchase. As you sit down together to factor in the deferred payments, it may become evident that although one or both of you really want an item, it just isn't financially possible at this time. You may discover as the years pass that the magic amount increases which requires mutual agreement before the purchase is made. We started out at $5.00 (this was the old days when five dollars was worth something!). Before long our financial picture had changed and we raised the ceiling to $50.00. It went from there to $250.00, then to $500.00. We discovered that too many really good deals were being missed because we had to find a time to sit down and discuss the purchase. You will soon discover whether one or both of you have good financial sense. Our limit is now at $5000.00 and often a quick phone call is all that is necessary to make the decision. I don't know if we will ever get to the point where money is no concern. It adds to our sense of "team" when we consult with each other over these issues. It all but eliminated the "I" problems in the financial arena.

Equally as dangerous as the financial problems caused by "I" problems are those resulting from making plans without consulting. When the valuable and limited resource of time is squandered by impulse commitments, the risk of marital conflict escalates. I have probably caused more stress in our marriage over this area than any other I am aware of. During the early years of marriage, having been all but totally independent all of my adult life, it was difficult to remember to check in before making commitments. There were too many tears shed those first few years because we didn't take time to keep each other informed about our plans.

The solution is simple. Every morning we sit down and "calendar" the events of the day and as far in the future as we are aware.

Whenever a conflict arises, we have agreed that whoever planned far enough ahead to get their activity on the calendar has the option of either doing their activity or rearranging the schedule. In a single moment, the conflicts were resolved. As the children came along and started having activities of their own, they were included in the calendaring sessions. Had we not started the practice when we first discovered its necessity early in our marriage, life would be a total fiasco now that our children are teenagers.

I carry a planner with me that has duplicate entries from our family calendar. If I am ever caught without my planner, I tell those requesting my services that I'll have to check the calendar first before I can commit. No one seems to mind that I can't give a definite answer on the spur of the moment. Perhaps the subtle change the planner made was to constantly remind me that I couldn't think in terms "I" or "me" but had to think in terms of "we" and "our."

Yet another "I" problem becomes exaggerated when we see something that someone else has and want it for ourselves. It isn't bad to want something. The problem arises when we are not willing to pay the price to get what is coveted. The peace and security of our entire society is being threatened by those who see something they want and think that they should be entitled to just take it without permission or payment. Many older people look at the youth and wonder if they have ever been taught or disciplined. It seems that too many young married couples want everything their parents have worked a lifetime to attain, but they want it right now. Of course there are unconventional ways of getting enough money to purchase whatever meets your fancy. Robbing banks, trafficking in drugs, fraud, unethical business deals, etc. all promise "something for nothing." Those attitudes have resulted in law abiding citizens being required to carry the enormous burden of building and maintaining prisons by the hundreds.

We need to be mature enough to realize that accumulating enough wealth to buy whatever appeals to our eye requires time and effort. Window shopping, while providing us with an inexpensive and pleasant activity, has its hidden dangers. When you see the latest, or the best, or the greatest, and it is made so readily available, it requires self-discipline to smile at each other and move on to the next store. If you find that "I" problems in this area are causing you grief, change your activity. A walk through the park or a climb up a mountain, or a picnic near a stream are equally as rewarding as window shopping but seldom does one look at the huge, towering mountain and covet it.

There is another corollary to the "I" want pitfall. It is "If I can't have it, neither can you" syndrome. The senseless vandalism of private property by those who have not paid the price to get what others have, leaves one puzzled and disturbed. To this point we have been very fortunate. We own a cabin in the mountains. Every year a group of college age students break into the cabin and use it for a party. My grandfather, from whom we purchased the cabin, was a poet and wrote a poem about cabin etiquette, carved it in wood and left it hanging by the front door. The essential message is "go ahead and use it, leave it clean, and take your trash." The only way we know they have been in is that they leave one grocery bag full of empty beer cans near the front door.

The owners of the neighboring cabin are not so fortunate. Every year their cabin is broken into also. Some mindless individuals, after stealing what they want, breaking what they don't need, ripping and destroying whatever meets their distorted fancy, then defecate on the floor and smear it on the walls. The overwhelmingly powerful statement they seem to be making is "If I can't own and enjoy a cabin at my leisure, then you shouldn't be able to either." By far the more productive approach when you want something is to devise a plan to earn the money to purchase it. Keying cars, smashing windows, slashing tires, painting graffiti, etc. all seem to stem from individuals who are unwilling to allow others to enjoy something they don't have. I have often wondered what the reaction of the vandals would be if others did to them what they do without regard to the impact of their vandalism?

Unfortunately some couples employ the same tactic in their marriage. "If I can't have my way, then you can't have your way." Depriving each other of pleasures or preferences because you may think they are not meeting your needs, is destructive to the spirit of cooperation which is so vital to a solid marriage. Instead of retaliating for perceived denials, talk through the problem. You may happily find that the problem really does not exist. It is just another of the multitude of perceptual errors both of you make regularly. Those problems can be solved with little or not effort. Additionally, being aware of your perception is often sufficient motivation to a loving companion to make whatever concessions are necessary to maximize your pleasure or perceived need.

Other "I" problems that you may want to consider in some detail might include becoming so engrossed in your work or schooling that you fail to attend to your spouse and children. Being so focused on your own personal hobbies that you become a social isolate in your own family is also another major marital problem. The opposite is also true. When one becomes so involved in the circle of friends that the family and spouse take a back seat, problems are not far distant. If "I" problems carry over into family or marital goals, you are asking for additional problems. You will soon discover that your mate and your children are much more likely to support a goal (either long-range or short-term) when they have some say in it.

So why entitle this chapter "avoiding the wandering eye syndrome?" When the focus is taken off the companion spouse or children for any other reason, you are sowing the seeds of contention and possible dissolution in your marriage. Not to be aware of them would only make the break-up of your marriage that much more of a bitter pill to swallow. Now having been warned, we will move on to the next topic hoping that you are more wise than so many hundreds of thousands of couples who have been blindsided by the wandering eye syndrome whose marriages have fallen victim to the dreaded disease of "I" want!

20

RENEWING THE HONEYMOON REGULARLY

— ♥ —

Get out your photo album and together look back over the pictures you took while on your honeymoon. Does the nostalgia almost overwhelm you? Remember how everything seemed to be so rosy and ideal? Have those days necessarily gone forever? Part of the "hell" that some couples experience is to realize that the honeymoon was a renewable experience available upon demand and they just didn't take advantage of it. Too many older couples discover after the children are married and gone that they could have been having honeymoon experiences even while the children were at home. This chapter is to suggest different ways the honeymoon experience can be replicated frequently throughout life.

In the very early days of your marriage when only the two of you are at home, take time to sit down and plan out a number of "mini-" and "maxi-" honeymoons you would like to go on. The "maxi's" may take a few years until you have become more financially stable. The "mini's" can happen any time you can find a day or two to get away. Let's talk about the "mini-honeymoons" first.

Although the government is getting more tight-fisted and requires us to pay a daily user fee for the parks and national forests, the fee is nominal. While you are young, before the children arrive, a couple of days hiking and camping in the mountains helps life take on new meaning. The beauty of the surroundings rekindle romance and a real thrill in your marriage. If you wait until you have the time to take a mini-honeymoon, it will likely never happen. If you plan them into your schedule and then refuse to make excuses which prevent you from going, you will discover that there is plenty of time to enjoy each other. Surprisingly, the world still turns even when you take a little time to get away.

Somehow we always look at a honeymoon place as some far away, exotic place like Hawaii, or Europe. If you take a little time to visit the local Chamber of Commerce or a local visitor's center, you may be surprised how many sites of international interest are right in your own back yard, yet you've never been to see them. People travel from all over the world, paying big bucks to come see what you may be taking for granted. We certainly found that to be true with us. So rather than scrimp and save to travel great distances to enjoy a second honeymoon, visit something local. Does that mean you shouldn't scrimp and save for the big exotic one? Not at all. Save that money but don't wait to take a honeymoon.

Even when the kids arrive, traveling to the local museums, national forests, state capitols, etc. are generally short trips. But rather than include the children on the honeymoon, why not let them share a family vacation? you two plan and take a regular honeymoon alone. So you don't skip over what I am suggesting, let me rephrase it: "If the two of you are not continuing the honeymoon alone, together, the children may not have a family with which they can enjoy the local points of interest!"

Another source of honeymoons that are relatively inexpensive is the husband's or wife's business trips. I travel around the country (and occasionally internationally) to do seminars. The sponsoring organization takes care of my car rental, my motel room, and provides a generous per diem. All it costs me to take my wife is her airfare. In the day of fare-wars, we can fly almost anywhere for a very reasonable rate. Since my presentations only require that I be on task for a couple of hours a day, the rest of the days and the evenings are ours to enjoy each other. Although we leave our phone number with the kids in case of an emergency, we caution them not to give it out to others. We call them when it is convenient for us rather than having them try to catch us in the motel room. In the twenty years we have been doing this, we have never had a crisis that required them to contact us immediately. Occasionally they will leave a message to return their call through the motel, but it has never been a major emergency.

When my colleagues question how I am able to afford the luxury of taking my wife wherever I go, I explain that the honorarium I receive for the presentations more than pays for her plane fare, the car is provided, and we comfortably eat on my per diem allotment. The entire venture costs me nothing! I need to note that I don't make a lot of money on those seminars either but I don't do them for money— they are my excuse for yet another wonderful honeymoon! We have seen some wonderful places and done some memorable things during those seminar honeymoons. Most of my colleagues are now doing the same thing themselves.

If we had waited until we could afford to take the second honey- moon, we would have waited for a long time. Since I generally know a year in advance when these seminars will be, we can plan well in advance for family to stay with the children. Now the kids are old enough to stay by themselves. We have found that our appreciation for them and their appreciation for us increases dramatically because of these "honeymoon" experiences.

Occasionally we'll do a dumb thing (at least it is dumb from my perspective!). We will drive to downtown and get a motel for the night. You might think that is crazy to spend that much money for a motel room when our own bed goes unused. I think it is crazy too but I cannot argue with the results. The tension of day-to-day living is relieved, we share the sheer joy of being alone together, and the pressure of my wife having to fix meals is gone. Our whole life is energized by spending a few dollars to stay in a motel twenty minutes from home. It is difficult for my pragmatic mind to justify the expense until I look at the bottom line. Life is much more pleasant and problems are much more manageable because of our idiocy.

We couldn't have afforded that kind of luxury when we were first married, but we took "free" honeymoons (i.e. camping in the national forest, staying at our cabin, etc.) We put aside some of the money the honeymoon would have cost. In a very short time the accumulation of money from the free honeymoons enabled us to pay for a motel room when we really needed it. Some of our friends, when they heard of our idiocy asked how we could afford it. We told them we couldn't afford not to take the honeymoon! We probably only confirmed in their minds that we are crazy. Oh, well—then let them stay at home and fight the tension and pressure.

I have presented honeymoons to this point as being overnight, or multiple night experiences. We have also taken "mini, mini-honeymoons." These are just a couple of hours away with each other. Since my university teaching schedule provides blocks of time when I am not in front of a class, I can have my wife meet me in the parking lot adjacent to my last class. Then we'll escape for a few hours for lunch at a nice restaurant or even a picnic. The blessed phone mail (or cursed phone mail—as you may know) still enables students, faculty, and others to get to me. I faithfully return their calls—after I return. But I am a totally different man after just a few short hours. My wife says the short times away rejuvenate her the same as it does me.

The longer honeymoons take more planning, more financial backing, and more attention to family details than do the mini-honeymoons. Some of your plans may take years to formalize. You may discover, as we have, that the anticipation, the planning, the preparation were as satisfying as the actual trip. A young friend of mine took his wife on a cruise to Greece, Turkey and some of the little islands in that area of the world. He said they were the youngest couple there by many years. The older couples questioned them during the cruise about how they could afford such a trip so early in their lives. My friend and I had talked many times about enjoying each other along the way rather than waiting until the end of life's journey. Each of the elderly couples in turn expressed how they wished they had been wise enough to do the same thing when they were younger. Now they had the time and the money but their health didn't permit them to do all they wanted to do on the shore visits during the cruise.

It was another confirmation to me that without taking control of your own lives, you can soon discover that life has passed you by with all your dreams being tied up in "tomorrow." Today is a wonderful time to live. Of course there needs to be a sensible balance between "we can't afford to" and "we can't afford not to" take a big vacation or honeymoon. If the honeymoon jeopardized your financial future, then it would be foolish to splurge on such a trip. If, however, it only means postponing building your new home for six months, or deferring the purchase of your second car for a few months, then the decision is not nearly as crucial.

It probably goes without saying that a honeymoon is not just a mindless time away. Just as you dreamed and planned on your first honeymoon, so subsequent honeymoons provide excellent opportunities to fine tune your marriage. It is one thing to dream about the "what's" of life. What do you want to do next in your marriage? What needs to be fixed to make your marriage run more smoothly? What do you want to accomplish in the next few years? Questions like those should be planned and asked during your next honeymoon. However, don't feel pressured to fill up every minute with planning and problem-solving or the honeymoon will lose its mystique.

The real success of the continuing honeymoons is not only the fine tuning of the "what's" of marriage and life but the planning of the "how's." How are you going to effect the changes you want to make in the direction your marriage is taking? How are you going to get out of debt so that the interest is not eating you alive? How are you going to more effectively parent so that the emerging problems with the children don't continue to escalate? The "how's" are as important, if not more important, than the "what's."

I wouldn't pretend to tell you how to spend your next honeymoon. I can share what has been most successful for us. We generally do not tackle problems the first day. It is a day set aside to enjoy each other and the sites we are visiting. The romantic dinner, the evening alone are intended to help us unwind. After a good night's sleep we generally take the morning from breakfast until lunch to identify the "what's." What do we want to change? We have found it most productive to limit our heavy duty discussion to the parts of the day when we are both fresh and invigorated. When we start to get tired, the conversations quickly switch from the heavy duty problem-solving to the lighter, more fun conversations. We reminisce and dream more in the afternoons and evenings. Nights are seldom a good time to solve problems whether at home or on the honeymoon—so we don't. Remember, this is your honeymoon and you are free to use it as you decide to use it. After a couple of days of touring, site-seeing, and problem-solving, we spend the last few days just enjoying each other and preparing to reenter the battle ground of normal living.

If, during the problem-solving sessions, we discover that we are starting to become irritated or adversarial, we immediately change the subject. Who wants to ruin a honeymoon by fighting? Although it has never happened, I would rather come home without addressing any of the problems we are facing than come home with hard feelings towards each other.

We try to insure that we end the honeymoon on a very positive note. Why? Because if you end on a sour note the enthusiasm you have for planning and going on another honeymoon is lessened. We (I should say my wife!) tries to take enough pictures to remind us of the fun places we've been and the fun times we've had. We used to try to bring a gift or memento to each of the children and to significant others. That came to a halt in a hurry. We found we were spending all our time looking for gifts rather than enjoying the honeymoon. How many people did you bring gifts to from your first honeymoon? That, of course, is up to you. Maybe a large part of your joy comes from shopping for the kids or friends. If so, by all means shop. Occasionally, we still shop for the kids. It isn't because we feel obligated to bring them something. It is because we really want to. Let the honeymoon be your time together alone without the cares of the world to make you feel guilty because you are away from the kids or work or the normal press of life.

If your honeymoons are successful, you will find the excitement and fire of marriage will never grow dim. We enjoy our honeymoons now (p.s. I'm in my fifty's!) much more than we did on our first honeymoon when I was in my twenty's. None of the artificiality of the first honeymoon is there now. Now it is just the genuine enjoyment of each other. Sometimes I wish we had postponed our first honeymoon until we were ready to really enjoy each other. Of course that comes from a dyed-in-the-wool pragmatist and certainly would not be endorsed by my wife who is a wonderful romantic.

If you equate "honeymoon" with "money" you make a gigantic mistake. Honeymoons are times to dream and plan and enjoy. None of those can be purchased with money. Lack of money does not preclude you from having frequent, enjoyable honeymoons. For us, the continued success of a wonderful marriage is directly tied to the fact that our original honeymoon was only the first in a long line of bonding experiences where romance and love are rekindled and cemented. Has it been too long since your last honeymoon?

21

CONTINUING THE COURTSHIP

— ♥ —

One would think that the last chapter about honeymoons would cover the content of this chapter. However, we are striving to find every solution possible to avoid even the hint of divorce in your marriage. So in this chapter we will deal with multiple ways of keeping the romance alive between the frequent honeymoons suggested in the last chapter.

If you remember back to the time you were courting, how often did you think of each other in loving, romantic ways? Once a month? How ridiculous! Once a week? Equally as ridiculous! How about numerous times each day? That comes much closer to describing the way things were. How often do you think of each other now? If the answer has changed from the last response— many times a day—what has happened? Now that you've caught him or her, is the chase over? If you believe that, you are destined to be a rather boring marriage partner. The great fun of marriage is continuing the chase. It is more fun now because the dates no longer end by going to separate houses.

An awareness of how you won the affections of your mate the first time will reveal a rich seed bed for keeping the courtship going. Was it the phone calls at work during your break that let your fiancé know you were thinking of him or her? Would that be such a bad idea now? A call for no particular reason, just to say I was thinking of you, can have a very endearing effect. A wild flower picked from near the path you walked on your way home may be a meaningless gesture to you but may evoke memories of love and caring from days gone bye. Maybe something as insignificant as noticing something in a store window that reminded you of your mate sends a message with far more impact than the words you used to tell about the incident. All of these and a thousand other little mindless things sends that powerful message that "I still think of you often and love you a lot."

There are other little things that seem to go by the wayside after the honeymoon is over. Do you still open the car door for your wife? Or wife, do you still wait to allow your husband to open the car door for you? You may agree that it is a small insignificant detail but I noticed from an aged friend that he always helped her with her chair, opened doors for her, and even stood when she entered the room. I wanted my marriage to resemble theirs so I have tried to do the same thing.

Remember when you were courting and you used to hold hands all the time. You may have even had secret signs that sent the "I love you" message without anyone knowing what you were doing. Do you still hold hands? If not, why not? Over the years my wife and I have continued to hold hands. She maintains that at least that way she knows that one of my hands is out of trouble! We say that in jest, but in reality we enjoy holding hands. It would be dishonest if I didn't tell you that we have had virtually hundreds of people comment about our holding hands as a manifestation that we are still in love. We don't hold hands to send that message to the world, but if they want to look in on our marriage, I guess that's all right too.

Perhaps as young people in love you loved to surprise your girlfriend or boyfriend. Have the surprises gone out of life? Unexpectedly taking her out to dinner after a long day, surprising her with a night out to the movies or a play, giving her a single rose, or even sending her a letter in the mail just to say you love her. These are things a husband might do to send the message of love that becomes an endangered species if neglected. The wife can be equally as creative. Perhaps you might fix his favorite dinner when you know he has had a tough day or taken a taxing exam at school. Fixing your hair in a special way, or putting on his favorite perfume sends a silent message. Wearing his favorite nightgown or playing his favorite CD when he arrives home, or leaving a love message on his voice mail, all contribute to the continuation of the romance long after the honeymoon is over.

At times it isn't even a 'thing' that sends the message of love. It may be a look or a smile. Sometimes the press of life gets so demanding that we walk around as though the weight of the world is pressing us into the ground. Almost unconsciously we ignore those we love the most. Unless we take extra precautions, the hours we ignore our mate can evolve into days which become weeks, and then months have passed since we really expressed our love for each other. Unattended love, like an unattended camp fire, begins to smolder, smoke, and die.

You can insulate against such neglect by establishing a set time or event each day to act as a reminder to pay a little attention. It might be something as inconspicuous as the opening of the garage door or the reading of the newspaper. Every time you hear the paperboy throw the newspaper against your door, it can act as a reminder that you need to express love for each other. You might choose an event like the call to a meal as the reminder to fan the fire of love. It might be a time like just before you retire for the evening. With very little conscious effort, you can get into the habit or routine of expressing love for the one who is the most important person in your life.

If you have fallen into a bad habit of taking each other for granted, ignoring each other, or silently passing each other as you

162

move about the house, it may be a little awkward at first to break the ice and get things started again. You might consider using this chapter as the catalyst to get things going. Read the above to each other and then admit that you have fallen into a bad habit. After the floodgates have been opened, you may find that it is easy to keep the compliments going, to avoid ignoring, and to be more in charge of the love intensity of your marriage.

It is particularly important for the wife to verbalize her concern about being ignored or passed over. The reason I say that is because many men (many more than women) tend to be less aware that things are wrong in the marriage. They are more reluctant to get help, and more apt to think everything is going well. If you want your husband to be aware of anything—tell him. If you think he should be more sensitive to your needs (which he should be!) but fail to inform him, then you are sentencing yourself to unnecessary weeks and months of frustration. He should recognize when you have gone out of your way to make his favorite meal—he may not. He may wonder why you have arranged your hair a certain way; or worse, he won't even notice it. I guess the reason I am so keen on this subject is because it describes me to a tee. I have so many things going in my life that if my wife doesn't regularly remind me to pay attention to her, she could quickly get the mistaken idea that I am no longer interested in her.

There is yet another way of passing on a compliment. Wherever you speak good or bad about a person, eventually you can bet on it coming back to them. If you accept that as being a true statement, then why not put something good on the underground. Compliment her or him to your mutual friends, to your employer as occasion allows, to his or her extended family. Don't do it to see if it works. Don't keep track of how many days it takes for her to get the compliment. Just go on about your daily living and let the chips fall where they may. You may never be positive that the compliment got back to your mate. You will have the satisfaction of knowing that you did something that will eventually result in a stronger marriage.

If you want to be more creative you can call up the local radio station (which your spouse always listens to) and have them send a love message or dedicate a song to your mate. It is always fun to watch the reaction as they are casually listening to the radio and a love song is dedicated to them. If you have a little more money (usually saved a dollar at a time until you accumulate enough), you can buy a week or month on a prominent billboard which is passed frequently by your mate. I have seen several of those personalized billboards although I have never done it myself. I have often wondered what the reaction of the person was when they first saw their name and the love message on the board. I also once heard a page at the local department store for a certain woman. When she answered the courtesy phone, the store operator wished her a happy first anniversary from her loving husband. I really don't know whether the guy knew the operator or just wandered off while his wife was shopping and asked the operator to do him a favor. The wife seemed genuinely touched at the gesture of love.

Since I travel quite a bit, I have noticed signs at the airport welcoming a loved one home. Some of the signs are huge and require two or three people to hold them up. Other signs are small but seem to have the same impact. One creative young man hired a small plane, had a banner made and proposed to his girlfriend by having the plane fly over the park where they were picnicking. I would imagine that her answer was "yes" from the reaction of the people who were surrounding their picnic. With some thought and imagination, you will discover hundreds of ways of continuing the romance long after the initial honeymoon is over and in the intervening time between your mini- and maxi-honeymoons.

22

R E - E S T A B L I S H I N G   T R U S T

— ♥ —

It is an absolute truism "To error is human!" To believe that you can make it all the way through life without offending your mate is a fairy tale of the first order. There will be times when, in spite of your very best efforts, feelings will be hurt and wrongs will be committed. Those experiences can either strengthen your marriage or deepen the chasm of distrust between you. There are several keys to getting your marriage back on track if one or both of you have wronged or been offended.

First, learn how to be the first one to say you are sorry. Pride can be a great stumbling block. A few years ago there was a slogan which read "Love is never having to say you're sorry!" How totally absurd. Love is constantly being willing to tell each other that you are sorry. It is pretty obvious from both verbal and non-verbal messages when you have done or said something that has offended your mate. That icy cold feeling you receive from them is more definite than any words they could use. At that very moment, swallow your pride and say: "I'm sorry I've offended you or hurt your feelings. Please forgive me." With that, the healing process can begin immediately.

If you are the one who is offended, then soften your heart enough to accept the apology and set forth in clear terms what you expect to happen to complete the forgiveness process. Maybe a simple "I'm sorry" will be sufficient to correct the mistake. On other occasions saying I'm sorry is simply not enough to right the wrong. It may require time and effort to repair the damage. But if you are both willing to initiate the healing process at the instant the wrong is committed, then there is little or no chance for infection to invade your marriage and compromise your love for each other.

Usually during the early months of marriage, after the initial honeymoon is over, you begin to discover traits that grate on you. During the courtship days those irritants were often ignored or dismissed as not important. Now that the prospect of a long life together is becoming a reality, it seems more imperative that those irritants be addressed. If you agreed during the honeymoon stage of your relationship to identify and solve problems as quickly as they became apparent, this will just be the first exciting experience of fine tuning your marriage. If, however, you refuse to address the differences lest people think your marriage is less than perfect, you are laying the foundation for unhappiness and contention.

Deal with the exact issue that has caused the friction. Perhaps a young husband has offended his new wife by discussing too freely their intimate affairs contrary to what they had agreed. A trust has been broken. It is like a dam that has been breeched. If left unattended, the rushing water will erode the earthen dam and eventually wash it away. So it is with marriage. As soon as the first breech of confidence is noted, plug the hole. If there is an unwillingness to forgive on the part of the offended or a stubbornness to ask for forgiveness on the part of the offender, the problem only gets worse. Right from day one agree to identify, overcome, forgive, and forget.

At times young couples enter into a state of cold war against each other. "If he is going to ignore my needs" says a young wife, "he has had his last fun in the bedroom!" That kind of retaliation will rapidly deteriorate into a cold war between you that takes the happiness out of marriage and, unless controlled, will eventually result in the dissolving of your marriage. Never use your bodies or the normal privileges of life against each other. Don't refuse to eat together, sleep together, work together, or be together. If you have already agreed not to resort to such childish ways of solving differences, offenses, and problems, you will not be tempted to resort to such when the friction arises.

If a larger breech of trust has occurred, it may require a cooling-off period before deciding to try to resolve the difference. Wrecking the car may not be a really serious problem unless it is the final straw that breaks the camel's back. In other words, when compounded with everything else that has gone wrong, this final incident seems to push you over the cliff as far as exercising patience and understanding is concerned. Then it would be wise to postpone discussing how it happened and what you are going to do about it until you have both had an opportunity to reduce the level of highly charged emotion in your lives. It usually only takes a couple of hours to unwind. Trying to resolve the problem during that cooling off period could likely result in actions and words that would widen the breech.

There are varying degrees of seriousness associated with the breeching of trust in marriage, everything from the annoying little tic that used to seem funny to the ultimate breech. You may, if you choose, ignore the irritant and expect that it will disappear. Some actually do when they are only differences of opinion such as faddish conversation. Remember when "ya know" after each word was a cute way of talking? Thankfully, for most people, it didn't last. A few weeks and it was gone. Some social and verbal tics last longer and with time disappear without saying much other than mentioning them. Little gestures like slapping friends on the butt or "high five"ing are examples. At first they are novel and then them seem somewhat inappropriate. They are not life nor marriage threatening. The more offensive a tic becomes the more advisable it is to address it.

Some irritants are like mold. When you sweep them under the carpet of consciousness and try to ignore them, they don't go away but accumulate with interest, only to blow up at some future time almost without provocation. These are much easier to overcome when they first happen. Being able to determine the difference between those which can and should be ignored and those which must not be overlooked will take time and experience. You will know immediately when you make a mistake. Tackling the inno- cent, less offensive tics will begin to be viewed as being nit-picky. Ignoring the larger more important offenses will result in tension and potential arguments. It won't take a doctor's degree to tell the difference.

The ultimate breech of trust in many marriages that end in divorce is sexual unfaithfulness—infidelity. You promised at the altar that you would love, honor, cherish, and obey each other until death separated you. You promised to cleave to each other and none else. If one or the other of you have breeched that trust either in a moment of weakness or by engaging in activities which degenerated to the point where you compromised your allegiance to each other, then you have a very serious problem. Although it is not impossible to mend the breech, many couples are not willing to pay the price to do so. Therefore they separate and decide to try again with a different marriage partner. If your love was deep enough in the first place to be willing to try to repair the damage and try again, you may realize that a series of dumb mistakes lead to the fall. Unless you determine what went wrong and take steps to avoid a repeat performance, it will likely happen again. Even if you are able to repair the breech from a single episode of infidelity, the second may signal the end of your marriage. You cannot realistically expect to have your cake and eat it too.

For the vast majority of you reading this book, this problem (infidelity) will never happen. But the methods of solving the problems resulting from any breech of trust are the same. After admitting the wrong, there needs to be a change in behavior. It does more harm than good to say you are sorry only to continue the offensive behavior. The reason for quickly identifying and deciding to resolve the problem is that the problem never gets a chance to develop into a full blown habit—many of which are extremely difficult to overcome.

What if one of the partners thinks the problem is serious and the other does not? Talk it through. Unless the non-offended one can convince, without coercion, the offended party that there was no offense intended and that what was done or said was just an innocent gesture, then the behavior needs to be changed. On this principle there must be agreement. Unless you both agree that something is all right in marriage, then the person performing the action can live without it but the person offended by it will continue to be offended by the repetition of the gesture. Just an example to cement in your minds the principle. If you have agreed not to talk about your sex life with other people, and the husband or wife violates the rule, then in mutual discussion you both must agree that it isn't that important or the violator must cease from talking about private matters. The one who talks about sex can continue to live without talking about it but the one who is offended by sharing private matters cannot (unless they change their attitude) continue without stress while their partner violates their agreement.

After consensus has been reached, agree to forgive and forget. To continue to hold a grudge after everything humanly possible has been done to correct the mistake is to put the offender in an impossible situation. What else can he or she do to make things right? Unwillingness to forgive escalates feelings of frustration, anger, and the desire for confrontation. If persisted in, the offender becomes the offended and the vicious cycle starts all over again. Refuse to fall into that very destructive cycle of unforgivingness.

Next, forget. To say you forgive but will not let it go is actually another way of saying you have never forgiven. Once forgiveness has been granted, never ever bring up the offense again. I know so many couples who require continuing counseling who steadfastly insist that they have forgiven each other for the offenses the other has committed, but invariably when a disagreement arises, they reach back into their memory and resurrect the past wrongs and fling them in the face of their mate. With the passage of time, the arsenal of wrongs committed in the past grows. Before too many years, the weight of accusation resulting from the endless shopping list of wrongs from the past is so heavy that it crushes the strongest marriage.

One of the fastest ways I know of destroying your marriage is to dredge up the wrongs of the past and add them to the current offense. Take a long, serious look at your past. Have you fallen into the trap of dredging up the past to add weight to your present argument? If you have, isn't now a really good time to make a mid-course correction and refuse to do it again? When both of you agree never to bring up the past offenses, the volcanic eruption never is able to develop enough pressure and steam to blow even a pebble out the top. Although good memories are coveted and something to be developed, with regard to wrongs committed in the past, the opposite is true. The worse your memory of past wrongs is the more likely you are to have a successful marriage.

Even when the big mistake is made (i.e. infidelity)—or more precisely—especially when the big mistake is made—if you are going to make a go of your marriage, you must never bring up the past. If you cannot let it go, then dissolve your marriage! Wow! What a statement to be placed in a book about "Divorceless Marriages." Yet that is how important it is to let the past go. That is also how impossible it is to continue a marriage where complete and total forgiveness is not extended. I just don't know of a more effective way of telling you that you cannot engage in dredging up the past without dealing the death blow to your marriage.

After you have forgiven and forgotten and taken steps to insure that the problem does not resurface or happen again, then it is time to move on. Some violations of trust seem to leave us stunned and a little numb. The more quickly you can recover and continue living, the easier the healing process. The longer you ponder and mentally relive the offense the more wronged you feel and the more difficult it is to get on with life. Both of you have the God-given ability to refuse to dwell on the failures and mistakes of the past. By taking control of your thought processes, you can rid yourself of the temptation to wallow in self pity. Parties are fun but not pity parties. No matter how wonderful your marriage is, if you continually dwell on how difficult it is and how bad off you are, before long you lose your ability to see the positive and good.

What if another offense happens which is exactly like the one just forgiven. For example, you have agreed not to talk about your sexual lives with others and the offending mate violated the same rule again. Do you lower the hammer? Again, it may depend on the magnitude of the offense. If it is infidelity, the second offense may be too much to overlook—it may be the death blow to your marriage. However, to slip and talk about something we have agreed not to discuss with others, is probably not a lethal mistake. Remember, you are not to dredge up the past so this offense becomes like the first time it occurred. How many times should you forgive the offending mate for the same offense? Only you can answer that. The New Testament teaching suggests until seventy times seven (see Matthew 18:21-22) which is interpreted to mean as often as the offender sincerely seeks forgiveness. The hypocrisy of flippantly saying "I'm sorry, forgive me" without meaning it does not represent true repentance. I would be in serious trouble if my wife were not willing to forgive me more than a few times for some of the dumb stuff I have said and done over the past years.

For some reason I seem to be a slow learner. Some social "tics" have taken years to overcome. My wife would be the first to suggest that many of those social warts have not yet been completely removed. Thankfully, she is forgiving and willing to let me try one more time, and one more time, and one more time, endlessly. Someday I will get things right. Then she will be glad she didn't give up on me. Be very careful not to try to take undue advantage of this principle or you will rapidly be perceived as a "taker" in marriage rather than a "giver."

As you extend and receive forgiveness for wrongs, you will find that the level of trust you have in each other will automatically increase. It is difficult if not impossible to extend trust to the untrustworthy. Therefore, if you are determined to make a success of your marriage, you must develop the quality of being trust-worthy. When, not only with your wife and family but with your circle of associates, you develop the reputation of being trust-worthy, your entire life will take on a new dimension not previously enjoyed. Then your word becomes as good as a legal contract. When your motives move beyond the suspect level, you will sense a level of willingness by those around you to trust you without reservation—an unheard of condition, especially with the political circus present in our country. Someone said, "It is better to be trusted than to be loved." The older I get the more I am inclined to agree with that statement. Thieves may love each other but would be very foolish to trust each other.

Rebuilding trust is like lifting weights. You must start with small weights and slowly increase your strength as you continually lift greater weights. If a major violation of trust has been encountered, be patient as you reestablish trust. Start with small little things. Keeping one's word as to what time you'll be home, what you will do, where you will be at a certain time all contribute to the rebuilding of trust. As weeks and months pass and the violations do not re-occur, the offended mate will feel more willing to expose himself or herself to possible re-injury. Over a number of years, even the scar of infidelity can be eliminated.

It is important to realize that the offender is not the one who has the prerogative to dictate when trust has been reestablished. When we violate the trust factor of another, we lose our privilege of "calling the shots" in that area. We are not at the mercy of the offended one. If I have offended my wife, she only can determine when she is willing to extend unreserved trust to me. Learn to be patient. Seldom can we earn back trust as quickly as we think.

It is of primary importance to establish trust as one of the foundational building blocks of your marriage. Without it not very much good can come of your relationship. With it, the two of you become a unit that can withstand all of the stresses and pressures so common to today's marriages. Will offenses come? You can bet on it. Must the results of offenses be the weakening or destruction of our marriage? Not at all. The hinge upon which the door of marital bliss swings is the willingness to forgive, forget, and get on with life. Make sure the hinge is in place and well oiled.

23

TAKE THE BEST—LEAVE THE REST

— ♥ —

For better or for worse, forever or for a few weeks, you are surrounded by examples of the total spectrum of marriages. Whether a couple is cohabiting or were married in a huge church wedding, couples are trying to make a success of their relationship. With so many examples to choose from, it would be foolish not to keep our eyes open and learn from others. Life seems to be so constructed that no one lives long enough to have every experience personally. So why re-create the wheel?

How do we learn from others without appearing to be judgmental? To a degree we must be "critical" in our analyses. Since being critical usually has a negative connotation, we should note that to criticize is to evaluate both the positive and negative aspects of an issue. Can we criticize without condemnation? That is the premise we must start from. We (especially as young married people) are not in a position to condemn those who are further down the road than we are. I noted a serious flaw in my approach to life as I grew older. Before I was married I was an expert on marriage and child rearing. Then we got married. It didn't take long to realize that most of what I knew so well and could give advice to others about concerning marriage sounded good but did not work in practice. Therefore, I eliminated my self-assigned role as a competent counselor concerning marriage.

I was, however, still an expert on child rearing. With some degree of smugness, I would offer advice to young parents on how to discipline, teach, and raise their children. All that came to a sudden halt when our first daughter was born. What I had learned in psychology, sociology, and family development classes at the university required some skill to apply to an actual living, dynamic child. In fact, either through ignorance or lack of understanding of the principles learned in my college classes, I was unable to translate what I knew into practical application. Reluctantly, I withdrew from the arena of being an expert in child rearing. Now I was just like everyone else—just trying to keep up with the challenges of life. As I started to look more closely, I noted that many of the "experts" in marriage and family relations were either not married and had no children or were divorced. What kind of an expert can tell a person how to do something and still fail at it themselves?

So how do the successful either in marriage or child rearing do it? Observation and analysis are the tools to discover the answer to that question. Neither observation nor analysis requires an advanced college degree. As you interface with other married couples, watch what they do. You will quickly generate two lists of considerable length. One will be things couples do which you admire and want to have in your marriage. Another list, often much longer than the first list, will comprise things couples do that you want to avoid in your marriage. Identifying items on the lists is critical. However, don't be too quick to categorize their behavior into one or the other categories. Watch for the effects, the fall-out, the outcomes, the results of their behavior. For example a couple may constantly be referring to each other as "dear," "sweetheart," etc. but if the effects are not positive, don't automatically label them as good qualities. You may see a husband treat his wife in what you may call a harsh or abrupt way. At first glance you would label that as undesirable. However, the wife may be perfectly agreeable to that kind of treatment because she knows her husband well enough to look beyond the harshness and see the tender love he just doesn't yet know how to display.

Observation, therefore requires more than a casual glance. It requires that you withhold judgment until sufficient time has passed to see the results of the action. One of the serious problems we have in this country is our propensity to put labels on everything. Sometimes people label behavior as "abusive" when in reality it is acceptable to those involved because the intention of the "abuser" is totally positive. You will soon discover that much of your undesirable behavior in marriage is not due to your desire to be abusive but because you haven't yet discovered how to act more positively. Some of those skills which contribute to harmony in the marriage are learned only after many months of trial and error. If you label well intended but deficient behavior as "abusive," you may tend to get discouraged and want to give up trying.

As you watch others struggle to learn how to act in a more positive way towards each other, see if you can determine not only what they do but how they do it. Some people seem to have a knack of getting along. You might be inclined to say: "well they are just compatible." That is a nice, easy answer but does absolutely nothing to contribute to your being able to be compatible with your wife or husband. Watch more carefully. It might be that one thing they do is "never interrupt while your spouse is talking." Just that common courtesy can make all the difference in the world in keeping love alive during the marriage. To interrupt another may be interpreted that you do not value their comment or you hold yourself in a position of superiority above your mate. Neither may be true but that might be the way it is interpreted.

Watch for a combination of factors which contribute to the positive relationship the subject couple may enjoy. Perhaps they consciously include their spouse in on the conversation. Asking for their input, suggesting that they share a story or lesson they have learned, paying attention with their eyes as well as with their ears when they are speaking. You may also note that compatible couples refer in a very positive way to their spouse even when the spouse is not present. There isn't a putdown or negative remark which reveals their "true" feelings about the absent spouse. Combine that with a brightening of the countenance when the spouse enters the room. Any one of the above mentioned items suggests harmony and love between marriage partners, but combined they send a blaring message that these two really enjoy being married to each other.

Be alert, in a comparative but not condemning way, of the factors which are absent from the successful couple's relationship which seem to be present with the couples who are not so successful. For example, the couples who seem to be at odds with each other seldom if ever stand close to each other in social settings while the successful couples often stand side by side and frequently hold hands in public. That might be the kind of compare and contrast situation you observe. Another observation might be that the contrary couples seem not to be able to take a joke. They take everything too seriously even when it was intended to be in fun. The compatible couple, however, often laugh with and at their mates. They seem not to take offense at jokes because they know and have confidence in the good intentions of their mate. You may actually come to the conclusion that it isn't the joke that makes the difference but the confidence of the couples in each other that determines whether offense is taken.

I have noticed that compatible and loving couples give one another the benefit of a doubt if some joke or behavior is in question. Those who are struggling in their marriages almost always take the more negative option when a word or action is questionable. With a little more effort you will find a multitude of factors (usually appearing in multiples) which contribute to the happiness or friction existing between spouses.

Now to talk a little about analysis. Again this does not require a professional counselor's degree to perform. Take the lists you have made and see which ones "fit" with your personalities and relationships and which ones don't. Even in the very compatible relationships there are things I see in other couples which are just not something my wife and I would do—it isn't us! So as good as those qualities are and as well as they work for others, they are likely not to work in our marriage. Analysis requires that you know yourself and your mate fairly well. For example, I am very reserved in public about showing public affection (known to the young as PDA's—public display of affection). Some of the most successful couples I have observed are very affectionate in public. Although it seems to work well for them, I would be really uncomfortable in following their example. My wife and I have talked it over and she agrees. Therefore, we have not incorporated that "success strategy" into our marriage.

In looking more deeply into analysis, you may need to consider adapting the successful behavior to suit your individual personality. One very successful couple that we know talks openly about the amount of money they make a year. Although it seems to work for them and gives them status in the eyes of their friends, we have decided to talk more about the things we are doing and the places we are going. When we talk about our family trip to Europe and the fact that there were eleven of us who went (my wife and I, six children, two sons-in-law, and a grandchild), without mentioning the cost, people surmise that we are not on the ropes financially. It is just a slight modification but one that makes us both more comfortable than discussing how much we make a year.

Extension and improvising are also part of the analysis package. Sometimes successful couples do things infrequently that seem to be very successful. If you like what you see and the positive results which precipitate, you may want to do the same thing only more frequently and to a greater degree. For example, many years ago I noted what a positive impact it had on their marriage when an elderly friend sent his wife a single red rose. He repeated the gesture of love two or three times a year. As finances became less of a major issue in our marriage, I found that if I send my wife half a dozen red roses and a white rose, our really good relationship gets even better. It has such a positive impact that I repeat the gesture four or five times a year. It never seems to get old and always has the same positive effects.

Another couple who were sort of our role models when we were younger used to buy "surprises" a couple of times a year. I don't remember whether they had a set time or whether one would purchase a surprise and then the other would follow. What they did was more important than the logistics of how they did it because I decided to modify it anyway. As I improvised using a characteristic my wife has—she can't stand to have a package or present that she doesn't know what it is—I decided to follow their example. I would buy a little present, wrap it up, and leave it in the house with a note to my wife not to open it. I knew the anticipation would eat her alive. She would call during the day asking what was in the package. I would tease her that it was something very special but not to be opened until I got home. I knew from previous experience that she would not be able to wait until I got home. She would open the package, peek inside, wrap it back up again and then act surprised when I was there and gave her permission to open it. It was such a thrill to me and her to give her something in a surprise package. I modified and improved on my friend's practice to meet our personalities but the results were the same—it increased our love for each other and the solidarity we feel as a couple.

In analyzing the list of things you want to avoid in your marriage based on the apparent failures of others you have observed, let there be a caution. It is rather easy to identify the things we want to avoid. It is much more difficult to know how to avoid them. For example, too many couples fall into the trap of arguing. It is easy to say, "we don't want to argue in our marriage." It is infinitely more difficult to know how not to argue in your marriage. As you observe the negatives, see if you can (at the same time) analyze the contributing factors to the problem. I have noted that people who argue seldom really listen to each other. In fact during counseling sessions I will often have each in turn explain to me what their major gripe is. If I have them explain it to each other the conversation rapidly deteriorates into an argument. In turn I reflect to the partner what I think I have just heard. Often with a surprised look the partner will agree with what their mate explained to me. More often the non-explaining partner will say, "I agree with the way you said it but that isn't what I heard my husband or wife say." So I started asking the explaining partner if I had fairly represented what they had said. Invariably they confirmed my restatement of their position.

I have learned another caution. When we develop a mindset against an individual (even if that someone is our mate!), we hear what we want to hear and not what is actually said. I could say exactly the same thing as the spouse said but they didn't have the mind set against me, therefore they listened to what I actually said rather than what they expected me to say. I have found a majority of the time that couples really don't disagree philosophically. They just have different ways of expressing their views. They have fallen into the trap of making a summary decision before hearing any or all of the facts. That's what happens when you say: "I know what you were going to say anyway so why wait until you finished your explanation?" Rather a juvenile approach to problem-solving.

Perhaps to reemphasize that point, don't fall into the trap of telling your mate what he or she thinks or believes. Common, adult courtesy would dictate that if you want to know what they are thinking, you should ask. Observing how these dumb little habits start could help you both avoid a similar fate. Some marriages are so riddled with holes because of years of bickering that it is nearly impossible to plug all the holes. It is so simple to avoid the problems if you confront them early on.

Perhaps a final reminder on identifying the negative traits you want to avoid in your marriage. As you watch couples argue and disagree, you may become aware that it isn't about right and wrong that they disagree. They are not generally dealing with good versus bad. Most often it is merely a difference in personal preference that is causing the problem. Somehow when we fail to discriminate between personal opinion and right and wrong, it is easy to fall into the trap of believing that all of my personal beliefs constitute what is right and anyone who differs with me is obviously wrong.

Not infrequently our analysis of what is wrong in the relationships of others is also wrong. Life is really complex. Too often we try to find simple solutions to very complex problems. It is wise to take time to really think through what we have determined to be the flaws in the marriages we have observed. See if there may be other contributing factors which bear more weight on the negative outcome than your obvious, first impression. For instance, arguing can simplistically be caused from not listening to what the other is really saying. Perhaps a deeper analysis might reveal that there is no genuine trust between the warring partners, therefore they always assume that what the other is proposing has a hidden, sinister motive. I have tried to stand back and listen to conversations between my wife and me. If I did not trust her implicitly, I might be tempted to be offended. But I know her heart and no matter what the words say, I know that she is not saying anything that would hurt my feelings or put me down. The trust issue, as mentioned in a previous chapter, is the real discrimination between taking offense in marriage and not.

Learning from others is helpful and time saving. Avoiding similar mistakes saves us months and years of anguish and heartache as we sidestep the pitfalls so many couples fall into. Life is difficult at best but when we insist on shooting ourselves in the foot by repeating the mistakes of the past and failing to take full advantage of the lessons others have painfully learned, it makes life almost impossible. So learn the good, beneficial, productive, solidifying "tricks of the trade" from the successful. Avoid like a plague the bad, divisive, marriage-weakening faults of the unsuccessful. Live above the mistakes and enjoy the ride through the marital tunnel of love.

24

AVOIDING EXTREMES

— ♥ —

In jest at a party, a friend once said: "Anything worth doing is worth doing to excess!" Although it was funny because everyone understood that it was not intended to be taken seriously, it is not funny in marriage. Moderation is a far safer road to follow. If you look at moderation as the centerline of a road and extremes as the shoulders of the road, you can see that you are less likely to wreck into a fence or barrow pit if you stay in the middle of the road than if you see how closely you can drive to the edges of the road.

It is important to avoid using descriptions in your conversations with your spouse that include the extremes. It is generally in the extremes that patience is tried, angry words are exchanged, and problems are blown out of proportion: Accusations like "You always put me down!" or "You never treat me with thoughtfulness and consideration!" often evoke feelings of anger and betrayal rather than providing an opportunity to solve a problem. The one being accused, does not believe that they always put the accuser down. They can probably think of many times when they have used thoughtfulness and consideration in their treatment of the accuser.

The use of certain words should send up warning signals. For example, in school one of the clues to help eliminate wrong choices on a multiple choice exam are the words "always" and "never." Not very many things fall into either category.

Instead you can soften your words by replacing them with "I feel that you frequently. . ." or "It seems to me that you have a tendency to. . . ." or "On many occasions you . . ." or "Are you aware how often you...."Although the same thought is conveyed, it leaves room for the times when performance was not up to par but recognizes that at times acceptable behavior is exhibited. Although it is nice to firmly praise on positive attributes, the reverse is not true. As you try to take the rough corners off your marriage, consciously try to avoid condemning accusations.

Relationships are strained to the breaking point when childish verbiage is used to bully opponents into subjection. The threat to kill or do bodily harm may sound cute in a Hollywood movie, but just doesn't accomplish the desired results when used in marriage. Even having warned against using "always" and "never," I suggest never using threatening words in a marriage. If you are adult enough to be married, you should be mature enough not to use childish language to solve differences.

Boisterous verbal attacks on your spouse will only lead to heartache later on. Even though they may be viewed as "funny" at the time, too often tender feelings are hurt and erosion of trust begins. Making your mate the butt end of a joke only labels you as the weaker person. Saying things that are hurtful, even if they are true, without considering the long-range effects, does not demonstrate the maturity necessary to avoid the multiple pitfalls so common in modern marriages.

Having dealt with the way we speak to each other, we ought to consider the way we act towards each other. A friendly pat on the behind is generally viewed as an expression of affection. Taken to the extreme it becomes a form of punishment to the young and abuse to the spouse. Again, moderation needs to be exercised. How can you tell if your definition of moderation is not the same as your mate's? Watch their reaction to your behavior and it will become evident. If your loving gesture of a swat on the behind results in pain and a verbal protest from your mate, you can readily know you need to adjust the force with which you administer the swat. Abuse is not something the perpetrator can determine. What may be in jest, fun, or given with the intention of endearing, unless similarly interpreted by the recipient of your gesture, may be oppositely interpreted. When that happens—they are right!

Over the years I have been the one in the family who has devised nicknames for my wife and children. Usually they are funny and endearing. Occasionally, a nickname that I feel is really clever is offensive to the person I have labeled. Although the natural inclination is to continue using the name because of the reaction it evokes, it is very counter-productive to do so. When my lack of sensitivity allowed me to continue the use, I discovered that the person sought more occasions to be away from me. Since I want my wife and children to be around me, I soon discovered that it was easier to give up the abusive language than to give up the association.

I watched one of those ultra-uncomfortable situations unfold in the local department store during the Christmas Holidays. A man was standing in the endless line to return something that was broken or the wrong size. His son, who appeared to be about nine or ten years old, was with him. As they stood there the dad started teasing the boy by pulling his hat over his eyes. At first they laughed and seemed to be having a good time. Finally the boy tired of the activity and asked his dad to quit. The father, not sensitized to the feelings of his son, persisted. The boy's resistance became more vocal and more physical. By this time the father seemed totally oblivious to the fact that there were other people watching this rapidly deteriorating game. Finally the boy pushed at his father. In an angry response the dad backhanded the boy across the mouth yelling at him never to push him again. At that point the store's security intervened and both the father and son were taken out of the line. The boy was crying and trying to stop the bleeding from a split lip. The father was fuming that the security guard was overreacting. Those of us in the line were shocked at what we had witnessed.

Too often, in marriage as with the above instance, what starts out to be innocent fun escalates into a miserable confrontation. Until we learn to listen to and honor the sincere requests of other people, we will always have wars of one magnitude or another. When your partner requests that you stop some behavior or verbiage—stop it. You will not be losing face by doing so but will be strengthening, immeasurably, your marriage. Those verbal teasings and physical expressions of love are not viewed as abusive when they are performed in moderation. It is in the extreme that chances of a marital crash are increased.

Extremes are often different for different couples. What is extreme and abusive to one may be acceptable to another. If the lines of communication are kept open, and if requested restraints are honored, almost all forms of abuse can be immediately eliminated from our marriage. One of the areas where extremes seem to manifest themselves to the hurt of the marriage is in sexual behavior. Although occasionally a husband will complain that his wife is too demanding or wants to do things that border on being "kinky," far more often wives complain about the extremes demanded by their husbands.

In the spirit of this book, the solution should be obvious. As you talk through the problem, the offender must realize that he or she can exist without performing the distasteful act. The victim does not have the same options. If he or she is offended by a certain act, then to perform or submit to that act leaves them feeling cheap, used, and dirty. If the act is continued, then resentment, avoidance, and fear replace feelings of love and closeness.

It might be worthwhile to say that some acts which were distasteful during the early years of marriage may become commonplace and acceptable as the trust level between the two of you rises to all-time new heights. When the wife (usually) is completely satisfied that the husband is considering her needs and would not do anything that would cheapen their relationship, she often is able to relax and enjoy acts which may have been offensive to her before. Time and patience pay big dividends in the intimate affairs of marriage. Approach each other with reserve and caution and grow together into an enlarged comfort zone acceptable to both parties.

Extremism extends even to the movies we watch and the music we listen to. Perhaps you are aware how many in the older generation look with disgust at a carload of teenagers whose radio is cranked up so high that people for blocks around are forced to listen to their music. Other than being in poor taste and threatening permanent hearing loss, there isn't anything inherently wrong with listening to loud music. However, the apparent total disregard for the rights and feelings of others signals a far deeper problem. If a person wants to destroy his or her hearing, I guess that is their prerogative. However, to impose their personal decision on others signalizes a totally selfish person.

Marriage has the same possible areas of offense. While you may be able to hear your favorite group if the volume is turned down, it may be physically painful to your mate if the volume is cranked to the highest decibel level. On the other hand, you may be able to hear the music well if it is played softly, but your mate may not be able to hear at all unless the volume is turned up. With a little compromise based on mutual concern, both of you can have your needs met without going to the extremes.

Clothing styles tend to lend themselves to extremes. It seems to be to the point of absurdity to watch how some of the "rich and famous" from Hollywood dress. It is difficult for me to take a person seriously who dresses like a reject from the local circus. The way you dress makes a statement about yourself and your marriage. It is not necessary to dress in a three piece suit all the time to impress people unless you are working as a Senator's aid in Washington, D.C. Being sensitive enough to dress for the occasion says something about you and your mate. I became more aware of propriety and impropriety a number of years ago when I read the little book "Dress for Success." Color, style, and occasion all play a role on the choices to be made in the way you dress.

In marriage it is advisable to consciously decide on the image you want to project and then dress the part. A young man with brightly dyed, orange hair that was spiked to the extreme stood in a bank line in front of me a while ago. He was dressed in a way that was probably very acceptable to his peer group. Between him and me in the line was a professionally dressed woman who appeared to be an executive for some company. When the young man asked for a job application, I thought the woman in front of me was going to collapse. The boy was informed that the bank was not hiring. He left muttering some obscenity about the establishment and how discriminatory older people were. I listened to the exchange between the teller and the executively-dressed woman. Although I have tried to develop some tolerance and patience with those who are trying to find themselves, it was pretty obvious that the teller and the woman had not. They were very vocal about his joining the human race if he wanted to be taken seriously.

Figure out what you want. How do you want people to see your marriage? It is always fun and amusing to go to the State Fair and watch the different groups. Likes really do attract. The cowboys hang out together. The preppy group wander together and are all dressed alike. The business class look conservative and business-like. The glamorous try to look the part. The list is endless but the message is clear—you can't dress like a nerd and expect to be treated with honor and respect. It is easier to start more conservatively and slowly move toward the edges if you can than it is to start on the fringe and expect that people (many of whom are not very forgiving) will automatically honor your desire to change as you discover that the image you are portraying is not what you really want.

I would suspect that the point has been made. Extremes in foods, recreational activities, entertainment, etc. all have the same potential impact. Go to the extremes and there is a credibility price to pay. You may say that you don't care what others think. It is their problem if they have a tough time accepting you the way you are. While that may be very true, it is equally true that those in the more conservative establishment are generally the ones who are doing the hiring and firing at places you may want to be employed. If you are going to exercise your right to be weird or extreme, you must also be willing to accept the consequences which are often in the form of rejection by the establishment.

You might want to consider carefully before you take the extreme approach, how many fifty-year-old hippies you see riding their choppers around. They had their day in the sun when society took particular note of them. Then they disappeared. Most of them joined the ranks of the more conservative. A few refused to change and either became social isolates or became so miserable they destroyed themselves by overindulgence.

One more area of consideration before moving on to a new topic. Be careful in extremes dealing with religious worship. Most of the churches which are established and accepted are fairly center-of-the-road. There are a few which represent extremes. The "Jim Jones" experiment which ended in the suicide and murder of so many people was so extreme that parents were attempting to use legal means to rescue their children. Occasionally one hears of parents who let their sick children die rather than use medicine. Some do not consider that to be extreme but the courts certainly do. Some even want to"tempt God" by handling poisonous snakes to prove the scriptural promise that they would be protected from the bite of poisonous snakes.

Almost on a yearly basis, at the suggestion of a psychic or an eccentric prophet, people sell their goods, dress in white and await the return of the Messiah. Every year there are re-calculations by the "experts" on when the world will end because their former predictions do not come to pass. It does not speak highly of us to jump from one extreme philosophy to another. If the form of worship you choose to engage in is not clearly spelled out in the canonized scriptures, be cautious. In a world that cries for anyone who is credible and a solid thinker, you can quickly disqualify yourself from playing a major role if people perceive that you are an extremist in matters religious.

As I mentioned in the first part of this chapter, the white sidelines delineating what is acceptable and what is not are far enough apart that you should be able to "do your own thing" or "be your own person" without feeling too restricted. Society seems less than tolerant when we cross over the sidelines. Be careful to project or radiate what you really are and what you really want to be.

25

AGREEING UPON THE LEADERSHIP
OF THE HOME

—♥—

From my perspective, one of the truly tragic shifts of this generation is the adversarial nature of the husband and wife relationship. During the early days of colonization of the country, husband and wife were required to work shoulder to shoulder to make a living for themselves and a life for their family. Failure to do so resulted in starvation or annihilation of the family. In today's world it seems that certain movements have become self-appointed watchdogs to insure that the wife gets her dues and that the husband is coerced into taking equal responsibility for chores former assumed by the wife.

The tragedy isn't that the shift has taken place so much as it is the adversarial feelings which have been created between husband and wife. Is it all right to expect the husband to help with household chores? Sure! Should there be a more even division of labor since the wife often works outside the home also? Absolutely! But why can't we achieve that goal without pitting spouse against spouse?

As you begin your marriage, it is not only helpful but necessary that the two of you sit down and define roles. Some roles are God-given. Even if you decide the husband is going to bear the children, that isn't likely to happen. Although many of the traits which have been associated with the wife and mother can be polished and refined in the life of the husband and father, the wife still seems to be better suited to certain roles. Many men are more intellectually oriented than they are affectively focused. In English that means that a man is more apt to say "I think. . ." while a woman is more apt to say "I feel that . . ." One isn't better or superior than another— they are just different. In a recently popularized book "Men are from Mars and Women are from Venus" the author makes a definite case that men and women are basically different. To deny the differences does not eliminate them. To ignore them only increases the likelihood that problems will arise because a skewed perspective is applied to husband/wife relationships.

It is definitely true that not all men are logical and analytical (intellectual functions). It is equally true that not all women are sensitive, and feeling (affective functions). Some people insist that the wife take a very traditional role and none other. On the other end of the continuum there are those who demand that absolute equality in marriage is a must. As we mentioned in the chapter dealing with extremes, the more functional, workable solution seems to be somewhere in the middle.

By mutual agreement most of the conflicts of leadership in the home can be averted before they become an issue. We have found that being open and honest about our likes and dislikes has made our division of labor in the household chores much easier. For example, from the time I was a little boy I have enjoyed ironing. I can't explain it. My mother taught me to iron and we spent many happy hours with her mending while I ironed. Consequently, my love for ironing did not end when we got married. Conversely, my wife is not particularly fond of ironing. It was a chore that had to be done and she has few if any fond memories of ironing. It seems like a natural that I do the ironing. It isn't an ironclad rule. Many times my rather hectic schedule necessitates that my wife do the ironing. She is better at it than I am and so can finish the job much quicker. Even though it doesn't top her list of "fun things to do around the house," she does it without complaint.

On the other hand, I seem to be the kind of guy who likes the stability of knowing where everything is. My philosophy is "get it right the first time and leave it alone." My wife is one of those creative people who can find a hundred ways of rearranging the furniture to give variety to life. She loves moving furniture—I tolerate it. I have learned by sad experience not to expect the easy chair to be in the same place it was yesterday. I came home from work late one night and decided to unwind a little before going to bed. So as not to disrupt the family, I decided not to turn the lights on. I sat down where the easy chair had been earlier that morning and to my surprise and embarrassment I knocked over a little table with a flower arrangement on it. The noise of the crash brought the entire family to life. I sat there amidst the flowers as the family laughed at my predicament. I learned my lesson—now I turn on the lights and take a reading on where the furniture is before sitting down.

If she really needs or wants my help in moving furniture, I am happy to help—maybe a better, more accurate statement is—I'm willing to help. She doesn't become angry when I don't volunteer to move furniture, and I don't become irritated when she leaves the ironing for me to do.

Some of the basic leadership decisions which must be made if your marriage is going to be successful can and should be made by the two of you together. In fact most decisions should be mutual decisions. Where to live, when to have children, how many children to have, where to go on vacations, when to make major purchases, how much debt to incur in getting what you want. The list seems endless but manageable when both of you work together on the decisions.

There may be decisions that one or the other of you has an aptitude more suited for making the decisions. My wife is much more politically astute than I am. After she has explained the strengths and weaknesses of a political issue, I am able to follow her reasoning. When left to my own analytical devices, I am not nearly as insightful as she is. So before every election, she educates me on the issues and the candidates. Seldom do we disagree. If we do, I still vote my conscience even though I know we will be canceling each other's vote.

There are areas that I seem more suited to make the decisions because of my particular aptitude. It would be foolish to insist that I have final say in areas where my wife is more suited. It would be equally as foolish for her to insist that she make the decisions in areas where I have a degree of expertise. By being totally honest with each other, we have divided the leadership role along the lines of strength, always remembering to consult with each other before the final decision is made.

What if we come to an honest disagreement on a decision that must be made? I would honestly doubt that any organization could last unless there was someone with the final voice in a matter. Although it may not be a popular concept to those who want to re-invent the wheel with each new generation, I choose to go back to the very beginning when God organized the very first couple. After they had partaken of the forbidden fruit and knew they were going to be expelled from their garden home, the Lord instructed Adam and Eve on how things were to be in their new fallen condition (see Genesis 3:14-19). To the woman the Lord said: "I will greatly multi-ply thy sorrow and thy conception; in sorrow thou shalt bring forth children; and they desire shall be to thy husband, and **he shall rule over thee**" (emphasis added).

That would indeed be a curse unless one realizes that every-thing the man did was to be for the benefit of the woman. It is dif-ficult for me to envision a woman who would rebel at the prospects of following the counsel of her husband if everything he did was to enhance her image and station in life. It is in the unrighteous exercising of control or dominion that resistance is encountered. I am painfully aware that for the vast majority of the history of this earth, woman have been preyed upon, taken advantage of, and treated as second rate citizens. Many have been treated worse than animals, abused and destroyed at the pleasure of their husbands, and otherwise left at the mercy of the domineering male. There is no way that I can conceive that God would authorize such treatment. There will be a day of judgment when all of the wrongs will be righted and those who perpetrated such abuse will be made to account (and in many cases—suffer) for the pain they have inflicted upon their wives.

However, the unrighteous application of the principle does not negate the principles itself. Where there is power given there is also accountability required. When the husband is required to have the final say in a matter which defies consensus, he must be aware that someday he must bear the full responsibility for his decision. If his sole object is to meet the needs of his wife, then his choice would most often be to suppress his own desires in favor of the desire of his wife.

Great and wonderful things happen in a marriage when roles are clearly defined and voluntary conformance is exercised by both parties. Competition for leadership disappears, children do not sense a power struggle between parents because there isn't one. Bitter arguments and quarreling disappear because the areas of conflict have been eliminated. Tremendous mental energy is saved because the one mate is not constantly trying to magnify the role of the other mate. With the conserved energy, both partners can excel in their chosen and designated fields.

One of the real tragedies in health care is a thing called "territorialism." People suffer much more than they should because some doctor, nurse, or specialist will not suppress his or her desire to be recognized for the good of the patient. I work on an inter-disciplinary team dealing with the healing of the whole man. There are many times when one or the other of the five of us realizes that a certain individual team member is more suited to deal with the problems a certain patient may have. Because of a well thought-out, well worked-out procedure, conflicts based on territorialistic tendencies have been minimized and in most cases eliminated all together. That is why I know it will work well in marriage. All five members of our team are strong-willed, highly-trained, highly-motivated professionals. If they can make it work, shouldn't two people who really love each other be able to set aside petty differences and agree upon an action for the benefit of the institution of marriage?

One of the truly frustrating conditions in marriage is when the husband is unwilling to take the lead in areas where he is most suited. If you are reading this book early in your marriage, those areas may not be as evident as they will become later on. One glaring area is in the disciplining of children. Having raised six children my wife and I have noted many times how much more responsive the children are when I get involved. There is something about "dad's directives" which seem to carry more weight than when mom is trying to discipline the children by herself. I have probably spent more time counseling on this matter with marriages which are struggling than any other area dealing with family relationships. I would sincerely hope that the children do not respond better to me than to my wife based on fear. Force or coercion may bring temporary compliance, but will result in rebellion sometime down the line when children tire of being forced to do anything.

Dealing with persistent salespersons is an area that men are more adapted to handle in many situations. Over the years I have found it much easier to stand up, take the salesman by the arm and usher him outside when he has not responded to our verbal invitations to leave. I am sure my five foot tall wife would not have dared to use that approach. When creditors call, when problems with servicemen arises, when attorneys call and threaten legal action, it is often much easier for the husband to field those situations than the wife.

Although those situations are not absolute and in some cases the wife may have the personality and aptitude to handle them more effectively than the husband, they often represent the kinds of situations I am referring to. The key is to agree between you who will do what. If your initial assignment isn't working—adjust it. There is nothing to say that in a dynamic marriage changes cannot be made. The most important issue is that there is agreement between you and your spouse.

There are many areas where shared responsibility works well. To avoid frustration and angry confrontation, make sure you talk over what your expectations are. Be bold enough to state your beliefs and express your opinions. Then be adult enough to work on resolving the differences without threatening your marriage. Thankfully, there are few if any problems which defy solution. As with so many other issues addressed in this book, the fewer surprises there are in marriage, the less likely that the two of you will argue over misunderstandings. Take whatever time is necessary to identify and decide how you will share the roles of leadership in your marriage.

26

ALTERING DESTRUCTIVE FAMILY TRADITIONS

— ♥ —

Families are great! I don't know what we would do without them. They provide, in many instances, a good portion of our identity. If you hadn't had someone to nurture you as an infant, you wouldn't be reading this book. Many of the first lessons of life were learned from our families. Even if you didn't come from the ideal family (which very few did!) we are still indebted to our families for our beginning. Now, having said that, let's turn to the subject of this chapter.

Many families have developed over generations specific traditions for handling almost everything. Some of those traditions have been thoughtfully considered and contribute in a major way to the success of the family. Other traditions are just there. In most families that I have worked with, there are some traditions that don't fit into either category—"good" or "just there." Some are actually counterproductive to the success of the family. Although we will discuss several of the traditions that fit into the last category, it is necessary that you and your spouse talk through the traditions that exist in each of your separate families. I may label a tradition as "destructive" in this chapter that you two determine is acceptable. I may not speak of some traditions which you two feel ought to be included on your list of destructive traditions.

Often the way that the husband and wife treat each other is established by habits or traditions that date back into past generations. If our genealogical records were complete or if everyone had kept accurate journals or family histories, we could identify who the culprit was who started treating his wife as a second-rate citizen. When children were born to that union, the sons saw the way their father treated their mother and grew up accepting that kind of behavior as "the way things are done." The daughters may have grown up expecting their future husbands to treat them in the same condescending way their father treated their mother. Another generation later, it may be just an accepted way of life for the males to treat their mates as garbage. The females may have accepted the role of being abused according to the whims of their husbands.

Unless broken, these destructive traditions all but eliminate your chances of having a successful marriage—one that is enjoyed by both partners. It may be that the men in the above mentioned example really enjoy their self-designated position of superiority. They may enjoy acting like a slave master, inflicting pain, everlastingly putting their wives down. Seldom, if ever, do they stop to consider how their wife must feel. If marriage is to be a mutually satisfying experience, some old traditions must be recognized and discarded.

Physical abuse must have started somewhere back in the branches of the family tree. It demonstrates a serious lack of refinement and polish for a man to inflict physical pain on his wife. If a person must resort to brute strength to get his way, he has failed to learn much about being a human being. Animals live by the rule of "survival of the fittest," humans do not. Is it necessary to use physical force to get your way? I don't believe it is. In my own marriage and countless other marriages that I have observed, reason and diplomacy work far better and with far fewer negative feelings than does the use of brute force. Resentment and hatred are fostered against the person who tries to force his or her will on those who are weaker or subordinate. If you want love and respect to reign in your family, you must eliminate forever the idea that using force is an acceptable method of getting things done.

Essential in the elimination of using force is the learning to control your temper. As you feel the anger thermometer rise, agree to disengage until you can get control of your emotions. It seems to go, almost without saying, that if you never become angry you will never resort to using force to get your way. Anger seems to be the little brother of physical abuse. As you continue to practice controlling your anger, you will find that it becomes progressively easier. It is definitely not a sign of weakness to walk away from an explosive situation. Almost every problem I have ever encountered can be postponed until I cool down. When you insist on solving problems in a highly charged emotional state, you almost guarantee that the outcome will be far less than you had hoped. Although you may gain temporary conformity to your wishes, in the long range you will be the loser. As your children conform out of fear or your wife or husband goes alone to avoid an ugly confrontation, you have achieved a short-lived victory. As time passes you will find that your children find more and more excuses for not being around you and that your spouse emits a much cooler spirit towards you. You are still in control because of your forceful tactics.

That condition may continue for many years. Sooner or later your children will distance themselves from you for good. They will come to hate the unrighteous dominion you have exercised over them for years. Your mate may reach the point of frustration where he or she no longer sees the benefit of staying married to you. They soon recognize that life is too short to live in hell. Then at the very point in life when happiness should be at its peak, you are left without a spouse and without the association of your children. At that point it is a little late to start evaluating what caused the total collapse of your life.

Hopefully, that kind of forceful abuse will never be something you have to deal with. In reality, with the violence which permeates the entertainment media and the news broadcasts, you must identify and make provisions for avoiding violent behavior or you'll be dealing with it firsthand.

Other traditions are not as serious and marriage-threatening as violence, but they tend to rob us of the happiness and peace we could otherwise enjoy in our marriages. If either or both of you come from a family where strong, domineering traditions exist, it will require some serious thinking and talking to avoid being overcome by them or adopting them in your new marriage.

Some of these traditions may involve the holidays. Does everyone always go to your parents' house for Thanksgiving Dinner? Is everyone expected to be at Grandma's for Christmas Eve? Does everyone in the family have to be at the New Year's Eve party? These are just a few; but, as I have noted over the years, they are also the very events which lead to hard feelings and family fights. What an irony! The very occasions which are supposed to bring us closer together, often drive wedges between family members.

As you begin your new family traditions, be careful not to be swallowed up in the enlarged family. If one of your families is very traditional, it is tempting to avoid conflict by just going to the prescribed celebration. What of the other spouse's family? Are they to be completely ignored? Many couples have been able to negotiate a compromise in the form of "we'll go to Thanksgiving one year with your family and Christmas at mine. Then next year we'll rotate and do Thanksgiving with my family and Christmas with yours." If the parents resist that kind of arrangement, the most stern stance would be to say: "We can either come every other year to your house or we will never come at all!" Faced with that ultimatum, most domineering families are reasonable enough to realize that having you there half of the time is far better than never having you there at all. Before you issue such an ultimatum, make sure you have both thought it through and are completely in agreement yourselves.

If a domineering parent is able to drive a wedge between you and your spouse over where to spend the holidays, it will result in the weakening (if not the total destruction!) of your marriage. Be sure you are so united that no one or no group of people can ever come between you and your spouse. Occasionally it will require that you move to a distant city for a few years before your total independence is established. Then, be careful, when you return, the first thing a domineering family will try to do is re-exert control over you. If you successfully resist their efforts, it will generally result in their treating you as a separate entity—which you are.

There are other traditions (or habits) which are not "sins" but can weaken a marriage. If one or both of you have adopted methods of solving problems which are not unity producing, it is to your advantage to identify them and take steps to overcome them. For example, my father (I don't remember him because he died when I was very young) would clam up when he was mad. He would continue his sulking behavior for as long as two or three months. Today we would probably diagnose him as being "clinically depressed." With apparently very little or no regard or awareness of the impact his childish behavior had on his wife and children, he continued his unacceptable behavior. I marvel that my mother was willing to tolerate such behavior, but they lived out their lives in a time when divorce was a rarely exercised option.

I have often wondered what would have happened if my mother and her in-laws (my dad's parents) had set him down and explained the facts of life to him. If they had laid out plainly the unacceptability of his behavior and proposed several possible solutions, would he have responded? I'm not sure, and probably never will be, because no one dared approach him. To ignore problems like these is a sure sentence you are passing upon yourself. People break habits and traditions when the possible negative consequences of their continuing the practice is adverse enough that they will take whatever course is necessary to avoid them.

One of the frequently observed traditions or habits is "one-upmanship." In some families the competition to best the story just told is so powerful that it makes having a normal conversation almost impossible. Many families are not even aware they do it. Generally, those who engage in the practice do not even listen to the story or experience being shared. They only remain silent awaiting their opportunity to interrupt so they can get on with their own superior story. Often words like "Well, that's nothing. Listen to this." or "That's child's play compared to what happened to me." are the prelude to their exaggerated tales.

What do you do if you have noted this practice either in your own or your mate's family? Make a conscious effort to break the cycle. Have a catchword that you use on each other to alert your spouse that they are engaging in the practice you decided to break. Consciously require that you ask two or three questions every time someone else is telling a story. That will reinforce them and more than likely will result in their listening more intently to your story when you do share it. You might even limit yourself to the number of experiences that you will tell in an evening. It is always more fun to stop while the audience still wants to hear more than to tell one too many stories. With some time and some effort you can break the cycle and develop the reputation of being a great listener.

Some families have established traditions of ignoring birthdays and holidays. If you avoid them for religious reasons, that is different than what I am suggesting. Often one person (i.e. Grandpa) has a big fuss made over his birthday but nobody remembers when Grandma's birthday is. If you have ever experienced with enthu-siastic anticipation, the approach of a birthday or holiday and then had everyone ignore or forget it, you know without me saying anything else the effect it had on you. If you are going to learn to live outside yourself, you need to respond to the needs of others instead of strictly to your own needs. Maybe your family isn't big on birthday celebrations, but if your spouse's family is, you had better break yourself of the habit of ignoring those special events. While it is true the special events mean little or nothing to you, it could be very destructive to your marriage if you ignore something that is really significant to your spouse.

Some habits or traditions are just a matter of poor taste. In a large family I observed, the children never used napkins at the dinner table. They always wiped their hands on the tablecloth. I often wondered what their first date would be like when they went to a fine restaurant and, out of a life-long habit, wiped their hands on the tablecloth? One husband I counseled with carried into his marriage the thoughtless habit of picking his nose and wiping it on the chair. He had a difficult time understanding why his wife got so upset at him. I suggested that the wife let him clean the chairs a few times and he would probably break the habit soon enough. She did and he did.

Many habits are unconscious and performed without the intention of being hurtful although they often have that result. Since you are trying to please each other, many of these habits can be broken with a little constant reminding—not nagging.

One of the most destructive family traditions I have observed is splurging to the extreme at Christmas time. Some families go so deeply into debt that it requires the majority of the year to pay for Christmas. The price of Christmas has been increased because of the outrageous interest rate charged by most credit companies. The most pathetic scene I ever witnessed was a young husband and wife who had come from homes where Christmas was a financial free-for-all. They had "maxed" out every credit card buying the best, the most expensive, the finest of everything for their two little children. On Christmas morning (as they both reported) the kids had gotten out of bed and made a beeline for the presents. They gleefully tore off the paper, stopping only momentarily on each box. After all the presents were opened, the kids took all the boxes and made a train of them. They played in the empty boxes. At that point the irritation level passed the threshold of tolerance with the husband and he flew into a rage. He screamed at the kids calling them everything from ungrateful, to stupid, etc. The kids were horrified. They were too young to understand why dad was out of control. He stormed off, leaving his wife and children alone for the majority of the day. It certainly had a chilling effect on the entire family. Who were the presents really for? The father and mother or the children? We talked things through and they made a revised plan for the next year.

I thought what they did the next year was really clever. Although the children were a year older, they were still very young. The parents bought two presents for each child but wrapped each present inside a larger box and that in turn was wrapped in a still larger box. When they had finished the wrapping, they had four very large boxes. The kids' curiosity was peaked long before Christmas. According to a Christmas Day telephone call, the kids had attacked the presents with the same gleeful enthusiasm they had the previous year. Box after box was unwrapped only to find a smaller box inside. When they finally got to the actual present, they were ecstatic. True to form, after playing with their two toys, the children lined up the boxes into long trains and played for the rest of the morning. Everything was perfect. The rather grateful parents exulted over the fact that they hadn't even gone into debt to buy the presents.

A potentially destructive tradition had been broken, a holiday had been enjoyed, and a burden (debt) had been avoided. This past holiday season I heard a clever advertisement on the radio. Two people were asked what they had gotten for Christmas the last year.

Neither of them could remember. Then one was asked where (or if) they had traveled as a family during the last year. Without hesitation the conversation focused on where they had been and the vivid memories that had been created. The advertisement was obviously produced and paid for by a travel agency. The point was clear. It isn't usually the "what" which leaves the lasting impressions. It is the people and the experiences shared which will stay in our memory. One needn't take a trip to enjoy an experience. The thrill the parents received in watching their children play in the boxes will long be remembered. I wonder if the parents know, even now, what they gave their children? Consider this tradition and see if an adjustment is in order.

Think carefully about those occasions that you really remember—with fond memories! Take the time to identify why those were good memories for you. It isn't always easy to isolate those factors which make something memorable. Sometimes it is the unusual. Sometimes it is a close call, or a humorous experience, or a spiritual feeling, or people you met, or things you saw or heard. It may have been a combination of factors, but something helped you remember that experience with fond memories above others which have been forgotten with the passage of time. Now take a few minutes and think about those times you definitely remember which are not good memories. What factors combine to make a bad memory? Armed with your two lists, you can now prepare to consciously engage in activities which bring good memories and consciously avoid situations associated with bad memories.

A word of encouragement and caution as you try to identify the good and bad traditions. The majority of the destructive traditions are more easily identified as the two of you dream and talk about what makes for an ideal marriage. Don't become defensive as you try to isolate those habits you feel should be changed. Often in talking of things through, you crystallize in your own mind how you feel about something. It happens, not infrequently, that as you try to verbalize your feelings you realize how silly something sounds. Often when you try to explain your feelings, you discover that the words you have chosen to express yourself does not convey the same idea you intended. If your spouse takes offense or responds in a hostile manner to an idea you are trying to verbalize, you will soon discover that you are more hesitant in sharing your thoughts next time. Be mature enough to listen without interrupting and holding your comments until after your mate has had a full opportunity to express themselves. Then ask some clarifying questions to make sure you are not misinterpreting his or her position. Take a few minutes to formulate your response. Use reason and logic to point out your concerns. Let your spouse respond to your concerns. As you continue your dialogue, you will see that the issues you are discussing become more clearly defined and more closely represent what you really feel.

Too often couples misinterpret the asking of legitimate questions to clarify their position as an attack upon them personally. Harmful, marriage-weakening traditions are not, therefore, identified and overcome because we "don't want to talk about it." If you both realize that even the most sensitive issues can be vigorously discussed if you stay on the same team, you can eliminate those stressors in your marriage which otherwise become the irritants sparking future arguments.

Take the initiative—establish traditions which make life enjoyable and memorable. Eliminate those destructive traditions which you both agree have the possibility of having a negative impact on your marriage. Families are great! Make sure your children can do this same exercise a generation from now and not regret being part of your family.

27

MANAGING DEBT WITHOUT HAVING IT DESTROY YOUR MARRIAGE

— ♥ —

Perhaps the saddest motion picture I have ever viewed was one I saw many years ago entitled "The Money Tree." It portrayed a young couple, so in love, who got married and immediately fell into the easy credit trap. Everything they wanted was available for "Zero down, nothing to pay for six months!" It sounded too good to be true—It **was** too good to be true. When the six months had expired of interest free use of the item, the bill collector was right there. The accumulation of bills became overwhelming. The movie ended with the young wife and mother taking the baby to return to live with her parents. The final scene was a repossessing of the bed, leaving an empty apartment with the distraught husband sitting alone on the floor. His life was ruined. His world had collapsed. All of this had resulted from their unbridled desire to have everything their parents had without waiting until they could afford it.

It is not my intention to lecture you on how to spend your money. It is my desire to help you avoid repeating the above scenario which is played out daily in too many homes. Let's discuss some of the basic sound principles leading to financial stability. Some are so obvious that you may wonder why I even mention them. I wouldn't bring them up if lives were not being ruined because of ignoring the principles.

First, the most stress free way of living (financially) is to spend less than you make! Pretty obvious. If you find that you are not living within your means, there are only two options available to you. 1) Increase your income, or 2) decrease your outgo. I guess you could include a third which would be a combination of the two options.

If you decide you need to increase your income, you have many more options than you might initially suspect. Most young people think in terms of "getting a second job." Although that is certainly a viable option and one that is frequently employed, it has obvious limitations. How many full time jobs can you hold down? If you want to work every waking hour, you can hold down two! Three eight-hour jobs per day is a physical impossibility. Another option for increasing your income is to have both husband and wife work. That has a positive and a negative side to it.

If both of you work, you will find that two paychecks really do go further than one. However, if you decide to start your family and you mutually agree that the wife will stay home and take care of the baby, are you shooting yourself in the foot by getting accustomed to living on two incomes? What will happen when the wife's paycheck no longer comes in? Can you meet the normal bills?

I think we were probably not smart enough to have thought of it ourselves when we were first married, but someone must have given us the idea to learn to live on my income, even though my wife worked over a year after we were first married. We banked her total paycheck. When our first child arrived and my wife quit work—no big deal. We were not accustomed to living on her income anyway. The other unanticipated blessing that came was that we were able to make the down payment on a second home from the money we had saved from my wife's employment.

That actually brings me to a second way of increasing your income. We obviously did not need two homes to live in. We rented out the home we just purchased. The rental payments were higher than our mortgage payment. Therefore, without me working any longer hours, we had additional money coming in every month. Again, we decided not to get in a situation where we had to have that income to survive. We banked the surplus rent money. It was a good thing we did. We were so naive that we hadn't considered fire insurance, taxes, and repair bills. Had we spent every dime as it came in, we would have been forced to take out bankruptcy and probably would have lost both our houses. As we continued to save and were more alert to perform preventative maintenance, we saw that we were actually saving more money than the second home was requiring.

You will rapidly learn that with the limited hours in the day, it would be preferable to do something with your resources other than "dollar an hour" work. By that I mean, no matter what your hourly wage may be, if you don't put in the time, you don't earn the money. You may earn $100 an hour and feel you have arrived. That would be good until the day you can no longer put in any time. Then your $100-an-hour job ends. See if you can start young by postponing the urge to have everything right now. Defer the luxuries until you have developed and implemented a plan to have others work for you. It doesn't require a doctor's degree in business administration nor does it require thousands of dollars to start your own business. Consider just a couple of examples. You can buy a power lawn mower for a couple of hundred dollars. Then hire the kid down the street for $2.00 an hour. Charge $10.00 per lawn. Each lawn may take an hour. It sounds like you make $8.00 for each lawn. Not exactly! You must pay for the mower, put gas into it, maintain it, and save money for a replacement mower. You might not make $8.00 per lawn but you might easily make $4.00. As long as there are lawns to mow and kids that need work, you have an almost guaranteed income.

In the winter, you might either buy a snow blower or buy a couple of snow shovels. Then do the same things. Although these are very basic ideas, your creativity will probably come up with a dozen more good ideas which could put other people to work for you. Virtually the only limit on how many businesses you can be either sole owner of or joint partners in, is how much time and energy you care to invest. If your goal is to enrich those who work for you, you will rapidly find that you can make a lot of money yourself.

So as not to miss emphasizing what I consider one of the soundest financial principles, let me revisit it for just a minute. Don't get accustomed to living on two wages if there is a possibility that one of the wage earners will be eliminated from the work force at a future date.

The second way of balancing your budget is to decrease the outgo. You will find that there are certain fixed expenses which cannot be decreased! Not a true statement! If you find yourselves in an apartment that is beyond your means, you can move to a smaller, more modest apartment. Your car may be great and the envy of your entire circle of friends, but may be strapping your financially. Either public transportation or a smaller, more economical car may greatly reduce the monthly car payment, gas, and maintenance bills. Even your utility bills can be trimmed by thinking and acting smarter. Lights can be turned off as soon as you leave the room, the thermostat can be turned way down at night. Buying a heating blanket and snuggling under it all night is cheaper (and more fun!) than heating the entire apartment. Taking shorter showers or turning off the water while you soap up, can cut down on your gas bill. Learning to fix meals from scratch rather than buying pre-prepared meals can greatly reduce your grocery bill. Renting a video rather than going to a movie saves considerable money. Calculating the "break-even" point with an expert can help you determine if a larger deductible on your insurance could substantially reduce your premium. These are just a few of the considerations you can look at when you are trying to decrease the outgo.

Although very important, I am going to leave those two concepts (i.e. increasing your income or decreasing your outgo) and focus on one of the great stressors in today's living—credit card buying! It is appalling if not criminal how credit companies make "easy money" available to untrained, uninformed, and unwary customers. Almost the entirety of modern advertising is centered around the buy-now-pay-later ploy. Another "come on" which is very popular is buy now and get some fantastic thing or trip free.

If a young couple would stand back and ask a simple question, most of the hype could be dispelled. The question is: "If we were the owners of the company, could we literally afford to give away free everything they are offering?" Even without a degree in finance, the average person can see that companies would not be able to stay in business if they gave their promotional item away without some means of recovering their investment.

Many people are buying houses and cars that they never intend on paying off. They purchase with the idea that the economy will collapse before their payments are due. Living on the edge is not illegal although time has proven that it isn't a wise practice. Legal or not, living on the fringe does not contribute to a stable, stress-free marriage. In the example cited at the beginning of this chapter, the major contributing factor to the breakup of the young couple's marriage was their unwise spending. Companies who prey on the young couples seem to have no regard for the destructive impact their credit will have on the individuals. The almighty dollar holds sway in spite of the trail of broken lives that is left in its wake.

How can you avoid the credit card trap? Some will argue that it is necessary to establish a credit history so that when you purchase a car or a home or a major appliance, you can be approved without all the hassle. It is true that the financial world seems to gang up to force you into accepting purchases on credit. It is not true that you must plunge hopelessly into debt in order to establish credit. There is a simple solution. Buy something on credit. Take the money you would normally have used to pay for the item and put it into your savings account in the bank. As the payments become due, make the payment. It is the payment history the future lenders are interested in, not how much you borrowed or how much interest you paid. After you have paid the payments (which includes the payment for the item plus the interest they charge on the money they advanced you) for a number of months, take the money out of the bank and pay off the balance. While it is true that the interest rate you are paying for the installment purchase is much higher than the interest the bank pays you on your money in savings, it seems to be the price you must pay to establish a credit history.

After you have done that a few times, you have a history and buying a car, house, major appliance should be much easier. I don't remember anything as financially discouraging as the first time we used a credit card to purchase gas. When we submitted our travel expenses (because our travel was business related), the reimbursement check came. We were elated with the extra cash until the credit card bill came. Almost the entire travel reimbursement check was already spent. How discouraging! Although we continued to use the credit card, we started taking the surplus from the travel reimbursement check and paying towards the next month's bill. Before long we were a month ahead. Because we paid off the credit card bill by the "due date" we were charged no interest. Therefore it was like the credit card company financing our gas for the entire month. Not to feel badly for them, I am sure they made their money from the service stations.

If you establish, from the first month you are married, the policy of paying off all your credit card balances each month, you will have successfully avoided falling into the credit card trap. One of the best instruments for young couples to help avoid the problem is a pair of scissors. In other words, be very cautious before you have a credit card in your possession. Unless you have been taught (or been burned a couple of times!) it is really tempting to buy an item even if you don't have the money.

If you are reading this advice too late, it isn't too late! Start today and set up a budget. The word "Budget" often has a negative ring to it. It shouldn't. It is merely a plan that the two of you use to take control of your financial world. As you list the total income on the top of the page and then list the expenses you have, it becomes a simple matter to subtract the total expenses from the total income. In finances "ignorance is not bliss." The fewer surprises you encounter, the less stress finances will create in your marriage. For a couple of dollars you can buy a ledger booklet at the grocery store or the bookstore. They already have lines drawn to help keep your numbers straight. Many book stores have ledgers listing the most common expenses so you don't overlook some and end up taken by surprise when the unexpected bill comes at the end of the month.

There is another area that deserves comment. That is the category labeled "Emergencies." You may say, "We're not going to have any emergencies!" That would be wonderful but it will never happen. The only totally expected thing in life is that there will be "unexpecteds" in your life. If you have made provisions for them, they need not be devastating. A tire is going to blow out, a dress is going to be ruined, a computer will break down, the car will need repairs, a tooth will be broken off, an emergency operation will be necessary, an emergency trip home because of the death or injury of a loved one, these and numerous others seem to surface at just the time when you are a little tight on funds. If you have taken adequate preparation, no problem. By designating a certain portion of the money you save for emergencies, you can start to stockpile funds so you don't have to use your food fund for emergencies.

Although you put a certain amount in savings every month, it is wise to designate that total lump sum into parts. Emergencies, family vacations, new car fund, Christmas funds, birthday monies, annually-paid taxes, insurance premiums, etc. all constitute categories into which you may divide your monthly savings fund. Then be very cautious not to steal from one account to pay for another. Although Christmas comes the same day each year, make sure you can meet your tax obligation by April 15th each year. Alongside each category in your ledger, enter the date the payment is due. If you allow for some fluidity, you can transfer funds from one account to another as long as you can replenish the borrowed-from account before the payment is due.

It is a real temptation and a very human reaction to look at the total you have in your savings account and wrongly conclude that you can splurge on some luxury just because the money to pay for it is already in your savings account. It is much more adult, and much less stress-producing to consult your savings ledger and see how many surplus funds really are there. If you are dividing your $600 annual car insurance bill into twelve equal payments, you need to deposit $50.00 a month into your savings account or you'll have a terrible bite out of your grocery bill on the month it is due. It is really tempting to see $500 in your account and decide you can take a weekend trip to the city. However, you need a plan for replenishing your insurance account within two months when the payment is due. You get the idea.

From the numerous financial planners I have talked to over the years, they all agree that it is wise to have some "mad money." Money that each of you can spend without accounting to the other person. It doesn't have to be much, but it needs to be some. You may be looking at your budget and laughing to yourselves—"that would be great but we just don't have any surplus." While it is probably true that you don't have a bundle of money left over after the bills and expenses, it is probably true that you can save a quarter here and there several times a week. The amount of money we spend on candy bars and soda pop is more than we realize.

As a young husband still going to college, I found that I could save part of my lunch money each day and before long I had five or ten dollars surplus. Those early days were tight for us like they are for so many young couples. I remember the look on my wife's face when I gave her a ten dollar bill and told her it was hers to spend with only one restriction—she was not to buy food for us or anything for the house. She was to spend it on herself. She went shopping several times before she spent any of the money. It wasn't the spending that made the difference, it was having it there if she wanted to use it that gave her a sense of real freedom.

Plan into your monthly budget some "mad money." Stick to your agreed budget. One young couple (who eventually ended up in divorce) asked if I would help them get on top of their finances. I agreed. On a biweekly basis the three of us would sit down and go through their budget. They were making plenty of money to get out of debt and live comfortably. Everything went well for the first three months. They could both see the light at the end of the tunnel and were thrilled at the prospected of being out of debt and having so much surplus money to spend afterwards. One night the husband came home with a new snowmobile. It was such a good deal he couldn't pass it up. In retaliation for his unauthorized spending, the wife went out the next day and bought a second car. Now plunged deeper into debt than they were originally, the friction grew, the accusations were plenty, the divorce rapidly followed. It wasn't that they couldn't have had their toys that destroyed their marriage, it was their unwillingness to discipline themselves and work together on a budget. If you fail to work together and plan, you have already planned to fail.

Working things out together is a must. Unless you are both willing to be financially responsible, you will be fighting a losing battle. Without question, more marriages shipwreck on the shoals of financial irresponsibility than any other factor. After the budget is fixed, stay with it for a few months. Give it time to work out the bugs. Then after six months or so, if the two of you want to revise the budget, go ahead. Mid-course corrections will be necessary for as long as you live. However, once established, be slow to abandon altogether your game plan. The better your plan the more likely you are to follow it. Be cautious not to make it so complex and cumbersome that it requires a CPA to work it. The most simple strategy that works is the best. If it is too simple, there will be too many hole through which finances leak out. If it is too complex, you will both tire of trying to make it work. Find your happy medium and stick to it.

Contrary to what many young couples think, it is not the amount of money you have that makes for happiness in marriage. It is how you use what you have. There is so much more to life than money and what money can buy. If you discover that your orientation is too financial, take time to reevaluate your direction. Time together enjoying each other and creating memories that will last a life time requires very little money, but a certain amount of time. If you end up with a bank account that would impress the rich and famous of the world and yet destroy your marriage in the process, have you really made a good trade? As you answer that question, you will clearly identify how "money oriented" you really are. Look carefully at the rich and lonely and see if the end product is worth the price.

28

CELEBRATING THE SUCCESSES

— ♥ —

Every few years we read about an expedition of adventurers who try to climb Mt. Everest. Very often the notoriety comes because someone is killed or some unusual occurrence projects them into world headlines. I often wondered why apparently intelligent people would attempt such a perilous journey. A few years ago after one such team had experienced a tragic fall of two of their climbers, the leader of the team was interviewed. I don't remember the exact words he used but in answer to the question why they had attempted the climb, he said, "Those who never climb will never understand the motivation behind those of us who do climb. Until you have stood on top of the mountain and know you have accomplished a feat very few have ever done, the effort seems out of proportion compared to the reward. Even if we fail to reach the summit, we have stood on higher ground than the vast majority of mankind."

I thought a long time about his words. That is true of mountain climbing but is it also true of marriage? To be able to stand on top of the mountain of life and say that you have a near-perfect marriage, seems like a dream. So very few people ever accomplish it. But if you gave it your very best try and didn't quite make the summit, you still are higher up the mountain than the vast majority of humankind.

Some will have read the principles in this book and scoffed at them. Some will see them as idealistic and not achievable. For sure they will never know because they are unwilling to pay the tremendous price to climb the mountain. If you feel you can't apply everything talked about in this book, don't feel obliged to throw the whole book away. Take whatever parts you can apply and you'll have a happier marriage as a result. There may also be the matter of timing. At this particular time in your life you may not have developed certain skills necessary to implement some of the principles. That does not mean the principles are bad or that you are inferior.

I took one of our sons out for a driving lesson a few months ago. It was his first time driving for a long distance. We went to the back roads in a rather remote area. We seldom saw another car. As he drove along this country road, I noticed that as he approached turns in the road he didn't slow down. After a couple of turns where I thought we might end up in a farmer's field, I suggested that if he felt like we were going to fly off the road while going around a turn, it would be better to slow down. I had hesitated saying anything for fear I would give the impression that he wasn't a good driver. To my delight, he thanked me for the tip and said he had felt uncomfortable driving that fast around the corners but didn't want to appear stupid by asking. How frequently we do that same thing in marriage! Something is uncomfortable or stress-producing and for fear of being labeled stupid or worrying that others may think our marriage is in trouble, we don't say anything or ask any questions. From that point on, my son and I had a comfortable dialogue about speed, cornering, holding up traffic, etc. He drove for over fifty miles and did an excellent job. He just needed to know that nobody expected him to be an expert driver his very first time behind the wheel.

Sometimes we feel like the only time we can celebrate our successes is when we stand on top of the mountain. If I were to climb Mt. Everest, I would plan a party for each night to celebrate the heights we had reached that day. Many young couples celebrate their "one week anniversary," their "two week anniversary," their "one month anniversary"; their "six month anniversary," and so on. Those of us who have been married a few years seem to have lost the enthusiasm for celebrating much other than our annual anniversaries.

Recognizing progress, even though the event is still in progress, is as essential to a successful marriage as getting a quarterly update on your grades is in college. You certainly wouldn't want to wait until the end of your senior year to find out if you passed "Fresh-man English." Why should it be different in marriage? Compliments, "high five's," letters and notes of appreciation are inexpensive but very rewarding. Looking back on that first year of marriage when so many adjustments had to be made, it seems like almost a miracle that anyone makes it through. Unconsciously, we took time in our marriage to celebrate each month as another "first." I say uncon-sciously because I'm not sure we intentionally realized we were celebrating. It may have been a mere comment like, "Did you realize this is our first Sunday dinner alone together?" "It was two months ago today that we got home from the honeymoon." "We have been married longer now than we dated before we got married." Each of these "wow!" statements just focused that we were actually doing what married couples do—live together in happiness and peace.

I remember when I called my wife one day from the office and asked, "Do you know what today is?" She thought for a long while then, after several wrong guesses, admitted that she didn't know. Exultantly I informed her that "You have been married exactly as long as you were single!" She gave me that incredulous laugh I have heard many times before as she said, "Who else in the world but you would figure out exactly how many days I've been alive?" It was a shared moment of joyful celebration. It didn't mean a single thing. It didn't change anything. Life still went on. I still had to work that day, she still had to tend to the needs of the kids. But for just a moment, in a very special way, we celebrated how much we enjoyed being married to each other.

You will find your own creative ways of celebrating the successes. When the credit cards are all paid off—that calls for a celebration. When you successfully pull of your first Thanksgiving Dinner for your families—it's time to celebrate. When the doctor confirms that the two of you are going to be three—party time! When graduation comes and a "real job" is secured—break out the sparkling cider. The list is endless. The joy that comes never ends.

How does one bring to a close something that is ongoing and exciting? I'm not sure but I need to conclude this chapter and this book. If you have not been able to feel the excitement and enthusiasm I have for my wife and our marriage, I have failed miserably. I would like to share a couple of pet phrases that help me stay focused on my goal. One is "whether you think you can or you can't, you are right!" What you believe you are capable of achieving in your marriage is probably exactly what you will achieve in your marriage. Don't set your sights too low for fear you will hit the target and be disappointed. Don't worry too much about those who mock and make fun of your attempts to have a perfect marriage. There will always be fools who mock and mockers who stand back in shocked amazement when you achieve what they labeled "impossible."

I like the statement "If it is to be, it is up to me." That summarizes a basic belief that two people can accomplish in marriage whatever they want to, but it requires effort on their part. Happiness and success in marriage are not guaranteed. They must be earned. But, like any other business venture in the world, if you play by the rules and put in the time, effort and resources necessary, you will succeed. Marriages fail when sufficient resources are not committed to the institution to make it work.

You must have a vision. If you do not have a dream of what an ideal marriage is, how will you know when you have arrived? I readily admit that my vision is a composite of many couples I have observed over a lifetime. My vision is constantly changing as I mature and realize that some of my "ideals" were less than perfect, and that with some additional effort, I can improve on what they achieved. I have discovered that a personal dream is difficult to achieve in a joint venture. A shared dream is much easier to make a reality.

It has become clear that having a well-developed, well thought-out set of priorities in life provides a framework upon which the rest of the journey can be built, without the stress associated with not being able to be everywhere at once and without being able to be everything to everybody. Priorities can save stress, they can also save marriages. Failing to plan and prioritize is literally planning to fail.

The world seems to be oblivious that "falling in love" is a misnomer. People grow in love through shared experiences and shared values. Falling in love is like falling out of a tree—you can get hurt badly if you don't adequately prepare for the landing. In addition, falling out of a tree isn't something you would plan to do on a frequent basis. Neither is falling in love something that ought to be taken lightly. Hollywood portrays love and marriage in such a distorted way that to fashion your marriage after what you see or television on in the movies is like embracing a cobra. It is the kiss of death. If you want to find success in marriage, turn to those who not only "talk the talk" but "walk the walk." Unrealistic expectations in marriage only amplify the problems and frustrations you will face. Whether dealing with sexual fantasies or financial dreams, being realistic will help keep your feet on the ground rather than your heads in the clouds. Believing that "once in love, always in love" signalizes trouble for your marriage. Marriage is like a campfire. If you take care to feed it properly and give it plenty of attention, it will burn brightly and provide plenty of heat and light to keep you safe through the night. If you ignore it, you will only become irritated when the smoke from the dying embers gets in your eyes and causes breathing problems. Keep fanning the fires of love through continued courtship, and you'll be pleasantly surprised that your love is much deeper and richer on your twenty-fifth anniversary than it was on your first anniversary.

From my own experience and observations, there is virtually nothing sweeter than a happy marriage. There is nothing more bitter than being married to a lover-turned-enemy. What has been written in this book has been written for the intent of helping you avoid the pitfalls so common to modern day marriages. Even the best advice will be of no value if you do not try it out.

I have given you part of my heart. That is always dangerous because of the number who may choose to desecrate it. However, for the others who are gutsy enough to give it a sincere try, you will enjoy what we are nearly three decades into achieving—a divorce-less marriage.

INDEX

— ♥ —